PSYCHOLOGICAL
EXPERIMENTS WITH AUTISTIC CHILDREN

PSYCHOLOGICAL EXPERIMENTS WITH AUTISTIC CHILDREN

BY

B. HERMELIN

AND

N. O'CONNOR

PERGAMON PRESS

OXFORD · NEW YORK · TORONTO
SYDNEY · BRAUNSCHWEIG

Pergamon Press Ltd., Headington Hill Hall, Oxford
Pergamon Press Inc., Maxwell House, Fairview Park, Elmsford, New York 10523
Pergamon of Canada Ltd., 207 Queen's Quay West, Toronto 1
Pergamon Press (Aust.) Pty. Ltd., 19a Boundary Street,
Rushcutters Bay, N.S.W. 2011, Australia
Vieweg & Sohn GmbH, Burgplatz 1, Braunschweig

First edition 1970

Library of Congress Catalog Card No. 79–124064

Printed in Great Britain by A. Wheaton & Co., Exeter

08 016088 3

CONTENTS

CHAPTER 1

CLINICAL AND EXPERIMENTAL
STUDIES OF AUTISM

INTRODUCTION

The basis for any study of autism is certainly Kanner's (1943, 1954) description of the syndrome, although the condition had been described earlier by others. Since his first clinical observations, other psychiatrists have used varying designations such as Goldfarb's (1961) Childhood Psychosis or Creak *et al.*'s (1961) Childhood Schizophrenia. Essentially, the children show autism, a tendency to ritualistic and stereotyped forms of behaviour, language impairment or complete absence of speech, motor mannerisms and inappropriate responses to sensory stimuli. Insistence on a fixed routine and resistance to change is thought to be characteristic, and islets of intelligence have been mentioned. Grossly abnormal behaviour frequently exists in the apparent absence of any obvious neurophysiological defect, and because of this, many investigators have taken the causes of autism to be psychogenic. Others, however, are more inclined to seek physiological causes because, for example, of unusual EEG records, and others again subdivide autistic children into brain-injured and non-brain-injured groups. The definition used by Kanner specifically excludes neurological damage, but symptoms of autism are accompanied by some indication of CNS damage in perhaps one-third of cases.

Clinicians have been concerned, therefore, with a description of the condition, and a discussion of aetiology. They have also been occupied with differential diagnosis, age of onset, prevalence and outcome prognosis, as well as treatment. Perhaps the only one of these problems which has been satisfactorily settled is that of prevalence. Age of onset has been determined largely by definition and by differentiation from childhood schizophrenia, but some lack of clarity remains. Some figures on outcome

1

are available and seem to be in reasonable accord, but international and interlaboratory differences exist partly because of discrepancies between different descriptions of this group of children, and partly because of lack of clarity about aetiology.

The purpose of this chapter is to summarize the findings from clinica and social psychiatry and to list the very few studies carried out by experimental psychologists. The justification for experimental psychologists to enter this field at all lies in the methods they bring to the analysis of behaviour. Behind their experiments are methodological presuppositions and assumptions about the nature of autism. What these are will appear as the work is described in this chapter. We recognize that the limitations of the experimental method, such as the absence of history taking, must be countered as far as possible by careful diagnosis, by working with a clinically relatively homogeneous group, and with different age groups. The advantages of the method, which are its careful analysis of hypotheses and interpretations, and its detailed listing and control of variables, may serve as a corrective to intuitive clinical impressions.

Because of the long-standing interest of psychiatrists in autistic children, and because this book is chiefly about experimental psychology, the following review will be rather brief. We are less concerned with the nature of clinical observations, follow-up studies and questionnaires about parental attitudes, than we are with the techniques and veracity of experimental methods. Another, perhaps better, reason why this review of clinical material can be brief, is that it has been well done by others (Wing, 1966; Rutter, 1967).

DIAGNOSIS AND SUB-DIAGNOSIS

Rutter (1963a) has given a comprehensive assessment of criteria of differential diagnosis, taking account of the views of Kanner (1943), Desport (1955), Anthony (1962), Van Krevelen (1952), Bender (1947, 1956), Eisenberg (1966), Creak (1963) and others. Creak et al. (1961) have provided a description involving nine behavioural criteria. As originally listed, Creak's criteria included gross and sustained impairment of emotional relationships and a background of serious retardation with islets of normal or exceptional intellectual function. These two items were regarded by many members of her committee as key points. The other seven were apparent unawareness of personal identity, pathological preoccupation with particular objects, sustained resistance to change, abnormal response to perceptual stimuli, acute and illogical anxiety, speech absent or underdeveloped and distorted motility patterns. These points were listed as characterizing the schizophrenic syndrome in childhood, but they undoubtedly describe the children often referred to by other authors as "autistic". Perhaps the most frequently noted feature is severe language impairment. Rutter (1966) notes that nearly half of all his cases have failed to develop speech. Of this group, many were mentally subnormal. Poor language ability relative to motor skills is well known to characterize mental defectives, as noted since Duncan's (1942) work. Rutter's control group, however, was matched for IQ and while showing speech retardation, this was far less marked in the subnormal than in the experimental group. This language disability in autistic children has sometimes been likened to developmental aphasia. Another characteristic commonly noted in autistic children is their tendency to stereotyped behaviour. This phenomenon, as noted by Creak *et al.* and listed by Rutter, includes resistance to change, arrangement of objects in straight lines and other fixed patterns, as well as a close attachment to particular chosen objects. Rutter has laid emphasis on the age of onset as a criterion in differential diagnosis. He sees early onset before 2 years as compared with onset after the age of 8 as one basic differential between infantile autism and childhood schizophrenia. One other, of course, is the presence of delusions and hallucinations in schizophrenics, and their apparent absence in childhood autism. Children who develop severe disturbances between the ages of 3 and 5 years are a diagnostic problem, but are more often likely to show evidence of brain disease. Rutter considers that this group can be regarded as often having organic psychosis, although as a group they will be somewhat heterogeneous. Onset before 2 years of age, or from birth, characterizes the genuine autistic child.

Lotter (1966) has considered whether there was a division between psychosis from birth and psychosis resulting from a setback at an early age. Rimland (1964) distinguishes autism in children from childhood schizophrenia. Creak *et al.* (1961) use "childhood schizophrenia" in a more inclusive sense. Wing (1966) and Rutter (1966) regard autism as only one of the childhood psychoses. Rimland reserves the term "early infantile autism" as used by Kanner (1943) for children with disturbance beginning at birth, whereas childhood schizophrenia as he uses the term, means a childhood disturbance with onset at not less than 2 years of age. He lists points on which research workers get opposite results with autistic and schizophrenic children, and suggests that, unlike childhood schizophrenia, there is, with autistic children, little likelihood of associated schizophrenia in parents or relatives.

Another approach to sub-diagnosis of childhood schizophrenia is that of Goldfarb (1961), who has divided his group into organic and non-organic subgroups, and found different IQ levels and different test performance levels in the two groups. He also found that the parents of the organic children were intellectually superior to those of the non-organic, although this difference was small.

A system of sub-diagnoses has been proposed by Gold and Vaughan (1964). This includes, apart from dementia praecocissima, infantile autism and the nuclear schizophrenic child, the symbiotic child, protophrenia, Bourne's (1955) deprived subnormal child, and Heller's disease. Although some of the notions propounded are speculative, these authors emphasize two things—the need to consider allied disorders and criteria of differential diagnosis, and secondly the variety of childhood disorders which have some symptoms resembling those of childhood psychosis. Their list does not omit forms of mental deficiency such as Earl's (1934) catatonic psychoses of idiocy, which sometimes simulate the key symptoms of childhood psychosis as judged by Creak's criteria. The same point has been stressed more recently by observers who describes behaviour typical of infantile autism in the severely subnormal.

While some investigators such as Kanner (1943) and Rimland (1964) regard the absence of an established pathology as essential for a diagnosis of autism (though not of childhood schizophrenia) contrasting points of view have been put forward. Thus Schain and Yannet (1960) in their careful study, selected a group of children according to the criteria of presence of severe behavioural disorders, including unrelatedness to people, onset during the first 2 years of life and absence of obvious motor retardation. Though their criteria fit Kanner's description, additional symptoms were found in many of their cases. From eleven available EEG records, five were abnormal. There were cases of microcephalus, blindness or cerebral haemorrhage. The sole autopsy which was available showed evidence of degeneration of cells in the hippocampus. Ross (1959) also reports that an autopsy on a child diagnosed as suffering from "Kanner's syndrome" showed extensive degeneration of many areas of the brain. This child had previously shown typically autistic behaviour, i.e. inaccessibility, absence of emotional responses and repetitive speech and play. Like many cases reported by Kanner, this one failed to give any indication, prior to the post-mortem, of any organic abnormality. Subsequent findings of Heller's disease and phenylketonuria after a diagnosis of autism had been made, have been reported. Amongst EEG studies, two investigations by Kennard (1949, 1953) and one by Taterka and Katz (1955) report abnormalities in 80 per cent of the records. On the other hand, twenty-one out of twenty-eight cases investigated by Kanner and Eisenberg (1956) had normal EEGs. However, Nesnidalova and Fiala (1961), Popella (1955) and Schachter (1958), all report abnormal EEG findings amongst autistic children. Fits and seizures are reported to have developed, subsequent to a diagnosis of autism by Bender (1961), Creak (1963) and Rutter (1967). Of Schain and Yannet's sample, 42 per cent had had a history of seizures.

There is something to be said for discussing collections of symptoms rather than diagnoses. From this angle, one considers both logic, statistics and the strategy of research at a point of intersection. If one thinks that a symptom is always associated with an identical cause, or very often so, then one's strategy should be to isolate the atypical situations and examine them before inferring that the commonly associated conditions are causal. If, however, symptoms or symptom groups can occur following a variety of antecedent events, one's strategy might be different. As both these situations can occur, one must be prepared to consider both possibilities. Additionally, it is sometimes difficult to get clinical agreement about symptomatology in psychotic or autistic children. This could be because each symptom occurs with varying frequency in disturbed children, and the likelihood of any group of symptoms is not so much universal as statistically probable.

PREVALENCE AND PROGNOSIS

One question to decide is how many autistic or psychotic children there are: two separate studies in England have produced a closely similar answer, Rutter (1967) and Lotter (1966). The figures were 4.1 per 10,000 for Lotter's and 4 per 9000 for Rutter's study. Brask (1967) also found a prevalence of 4.3 per 10,000 for early infantile autism. Other clinical and demographic studies have emphasized certain relationships of the psychotic child to his family or investigated his ordinal position in the family. All studies show a predominance of boys over girls, 2.5 to 1 in Lotter's (1966) recent survey in Middlesex, but as high as 4.3 to 1 in Rutter's (1967) study. Mental deficiency and many neurological disorders of children also have a higher incidence among males. Sex ratios in the Onondaga County Survey (1955) of defectives are higher than those from most other investigations, and show a ratio of between two and three males to one female at all ages. These figures differ little from those of Lotter's for autistic children. However, considerably lower ratios have been found in other surveys, and there is thus a likelihood that the male–female sex ratio in autism is higher than that for subnormals.

The question of the ordinal position of the child among his sibs is complicated by the relative completeness of the family and the age of the parents. Kanner (1954), Creak and Ini (1960), Pitfield and Oppenheim (1964) and Rutter (1967) all found a greater incidence of first-born children. Wing's (1967) material, although based on a sample which is more self-selected than Lotter's, shows similar findings with one important difference; the first-born of two sibs has a higher risk than in the other sibship sizes. Wing remarks: "There is no significant overall association with birth rank when this is classified into first-born, intermediate and last-born." The preponderance of first-born children, if established, may suggest birth injury as a possible cause, while a preponderance of later-born children is often thought to implicate maternal age, as in mongolism. Clearly, sibship position and maternal age are confounded. Among twenty children in our sample at present attending school, seventeen are first-born. This subject deserves a thorough investigation controlled for maternal age and social class.

Complications of pregnancy have been reported in studies such as those of Knobloch and Pasamanick (1962) and Taft and Goldfarb (1964), though these investigations would need replication to establish the validity of the findings. Simon and Gillies (1964) and Dutton (1964) have recorded delayed development of bone structure, height and weight in autistic children, similar to findings among subnormals; for example, those of Rundle *et al.* (1959), and Rundle and Sylvester (1962, 1963).

Follow-ups have traced children into early adolescent life. Rutter (1966b) has listed most of these and summarized their findings. About half of the cases were found to be in hospital at follow-up and only 5 per cent were in employment. Educational and social progress could be said to approach normality in only about 15 per cent. Autism was less marked in later years in some cases, but others remained autistic. Rutter found no accompanying increase in IQ where autism was reduced. Impairment or absence of speech continued as a severe handicap in adolescence in about half the cases. IQ measures remained similar to those found in childhood. Good outcome, where it occurred, was associated with an IQ in the higher part of the scale at 5 years of age.

AUTISM AND MENTAL SUBNORMALITY

The question of the association between autism and mental deficiency is a very real one. Wing (1966) remarks that autism can occur at any intelligence level. Nonetheless, most surveys show that there is a strong bias towards the lower levels of intellectual functioning, i.e. below IQ 60. Lotter's (1966) study shows that about 70 per cent of his probands had IQs below 55 (22 out of 32) and of the remaining ten, six were below IQ 80 as measured on the Seguin formboard. Three were within normal limits on this test, and one was above normal expectation. Rutter tested sixty-three psychotic children. Of those, twenty-six had IQ scores of 50 or below, or no reliable score was obtainable; nineteen had IQs between 50 and 69 and a further eleven between 70 and 89. Only seven children had an IQ of 90 or above. When compared with a control group matched for IQ, the psychotic children showed a greater variability on subtests. They were at their worst on those demanding abstract thought or symbolic or sequential logic, and at their best on those problems which required manipulative or visual-spatial ability or immediate verbal rote memory. Gillies (1965) found that thirteen out of twenty-eight autistic children scored below 50 on non-verbal tests; thirteen had IQs between 50 and 80, and two between 80 and 90. On a vocabulary test, four were untestable, a further twenty-two scored below IQ 50, and the remaining two below 70. No child achieved an all-round normal score, though some children approached or reached a normal level on some test items.

Goldfarb, using a slightly different terminology and somewhat wider criteria, compared twenty-six schizophrenic and twenty-six normal children, aged 10. Fifty-four per cent of the psychotics and none of the normals fell into the subnormal range with IQs below 75. Ninety-two per cent of the normal children and 23 per cent of the psychotics had at least average capacity. Sixty-two per cent of the schizophrenic group had lower IQs than the least able normal child.

The question arises therefore, whether psychosis in children is independent of IQ, or whether it is often associated with it. The occasional occurrence of autism in children of normal or superior ability might be similar to such specific disabilities as dyslexia or receptive aphasia, which may often occur in children with otherwise normal intellectual functioning. This question will be considered in discussing experimental work.

One factor peculiar to infantile autism concerns the social, educational and intellectual level of the parents. Lotter (1967) notes that from his survey it must be concluded that the parents of his cases ($N = 32$) were superior in socio-economic status, intelligence and education to those of a ($N = 22$) control group of subnormal children with some signs of disturbance. The difference between the social class distribution of the two groups of parents was significant at the 0.02 level, and the parents' education at the 0.001 level.

THEORIES AND EXPERIMENTS

Theories propounded by psychiatrists to account for childhood autism have concentrated on different areas of malfunction. While some have favoured a theory of emotional malfunction between parent and child, others have supposed cognitive or perceptual handicap in the child. Examples of theories of emotional malfunction are those of Bettelheim (1967), implicating stress in early mother–child relations, and Beres (1955), Knight (1963), Mahler et al. (1959) and Soddy (1964), referring to impediment of ego structure. Such theories, which often have their origins in those of Spitz (1945), Goldfarb (1961), Bowlby (1952) and Ainsworth (1962), have been criticized in their application to childhood psychosis or autism by Rimland (1964) and Wing (1966). The argument rests on three points. Few orphanage children develop autism. Secondly, no adequate demonstration of coldness or rejection in mothers of autistic children has been made available in the literature. Thirdly, the mothers of autistic children often have other normal children.

Concerning aetiology, Bender (1961, 1963) supports a genetic view, and Chapman (1957) and Kallman and Roth (1956) also entertained this theory basing their views on twin and sibling studies. No results from chromosomal studies have yet been found to support this hypothesis, though in most genetically determined disorders chromosomal abnormalities cannot be detected by the use of current techniques. Kanner (1954) and Pasamanick and Knobloch (1963) have suggested that the condition may be congenital. Psychologists such as Rimland (1964) and Hutt *et al.* (1964, 1965) have been more ready to support a physiological hypothesis and Ferster and de Meyer (1961, 1962) and Ferster (1961) have provided support for an environmentally determined view.

Psychiatric theories of perceptual or cognitive dysfunction have seldom been worked out in any detail. Perhaps the most notable is that of Anthony (1958a, 1958b), who sees autistic children as handicapped in the appreciation of sensory input. Anthony thinks that lack of object constancy and hence failure of object or word discrimination might explain some aspects of autistic behaviour. He discussed the relationship of psychosis and mental retardation, and also made reference to associated disorders, such as Heller's syndrome. Anthony (1962) sees three main theoretical explanations for autism in the work of his contemporaries. The first conceives of autism as a derangement of sensory input, the second as an interference with central co-ordinating and integrating mechanisms, and the third as a disorder of output. This categorization is general, and might correspond with a logically determined subdivision. However, the disorganization of sensory input and central organization is clear cut as a suggestion for a basic model of childhood psychosis. The autism of infancy, i.e. an adualistic confusion between subject and object as described by Piaget (1954), is the basis for this theory. The psychotic child has no time sense and his sensory input structure lacks hierarchical organization. He deals with the world in an *ad hoc* fashion without reference to history, temporal series, or spatial organization. In addition, he lacks language which, as Bruner (1957) says, makes it possible for a child to build a model of the world in a conceptual form. A confusion of sense input combined with a lack of language, could result in a state of autism. Much of this theory is interpreted in terms of afferent deficits, but interpretations in terms of central and efferent malfunctions are also possible.

Few psychologists have attempted to experiment with autistic children and fewer still have tried to account for their behaviour in terms of theories based on psychological experiments. The most substantial contributions to experimental work are those of Goldfarb (1961), Ferster and de Meyer (1961, 1962), Schopler (1965), Pollack (1958, 1960), Pollack et al.(1957, 1958, 1959), Lovaas et al. (1965), Lovaas (1966), and Hutt et al. (1964), apart from our own studies. The number of psychologists who have offered theoretical explanations of psychotic behaviour in children are even more limited. The most outstanding are Rimland (1964) and Hutt et al. (1964). Rimland postulated a deficiency in the relationship between consciousness and memory which might be determined by an impairment in the functioning of the reticular formation. Leaving aside the question of aetiology, this amounts to saying that the autistic child cannot relate new stimuli to remembered experience. This theory is derived from Scheerer et al. (1945). They suggest that certain children with symptoms resembling autism lack the capacity to think conceptually. Such general ideas are by no means uncommon in the literature on mental deficiency, where a supposed incapacity for abstract thought has been frequently posited. Werner (1944), for example, noted this incapacity and discussed it. Luria (1961) mentioned it in connection with his own experiments, and observation of the phenomenon has been a commonplace in mental deficiency study, because of the overlap of the concepts of intelligence and abstraction.

Most authors working in the field of subnormality since and including Binet, have observed the presence of *idiots savants* in the ranks of the mentally deficient. Binet (1894) wrote about *grands calculateurs*, and subjects with prodigious memories, always emphasizing that these abilities were apparently independent of IQ. One aspect of this phenomenon taken up by Scheerer et al. (1945) is what they refer to as the failure to adopt "an abstract attitude". By this they mean reliance on memory for problem solving, and little dependence on thinking. The authors reject Kanner's (1943) explanation of concreteness in terms of an emotional block. For this reason, they have no use for theories of failure of interpersonal communication.

Following this line of reasoning, Rimland (1964) states that psychosis in children results from a failure to integrate separate experiences. He suggests that stored material re-emerges unmodified, unlike the categorized store through which memorized material is normally processed. This is something of an inference from Rimland's actual words, but it is essentially what he means by "closed loop phenomena". His theory tends to explain autism as having a biogenic basis and as being characterized by lack of integration of input and store.

Goldfarb (1961), partly on the basis of observation, and partly because of the experimental investigation of children in his clinic, concluded that in psychotic children there was an emphasis on proximal rather than distal receptors. This has been justified by Schopler (1965, 1966) on the basis of evidence of the comforting effect of touch for young infants. However, the preference of infants for proximal receptors would now seem to be in doubt. Harlow (1958) was responsible for some of the evidence for "contact comfort", but Walters and Parke (1965) summarize evidence from several authors which leads them to conclude that visual and auditory stimulation occurring during caretaking, plays an important role in the development of social responsiveness. They are discussing children between 1 and 6 months of age. According to this view, a strong preference shown by psychotic children for proximal receptors would not simply indicate arrested development but rather a developmental anomaly.

Unfortunately, although there is much clinical evidence of supposed preference for touch, taste and smell, rather than for sight and sound, few experiments are available. Schopler's (1965) view that the structuring of sensory dominance is disturbed in autistic children as a result of sensory deprivation, has had little confirmatory evidence presented in its favour. Schopler (1966) compared thirty psychotic, ninety normal and fifteen subnormal children on their preference for coloured slides as against a vibrator, or their preference for a kaleidoscope as against a piece of malleable putty, or their preference for blocks which were coloured differently as against blocks with different surface textures, and finally on their preference for seen as against felt toy animals. For normals, an age factor accounted for an overall increase of total visual inspection, although time for tactual exploration did not decrease absolutely, but only in proportion to visual exploration. This trend was not always consistent from test to test. The psychotic children did not spend more time on tactual exploration than did normal children, but spent less time on visual exploration. These comparisons were made with chronological age (CA) but not mental age (MA) controlled. A comparison between the subnormal group and a normal group, however, controlled for MA showed roughly equivalent visual preferences. Schopler argues that this suggests that it is not the low IQ of the psychotic children which accounts for their lower visual preference scores. His view is that visual preference increases with age between the years 3 and 6. His results indicate, however, contrary to his own expectations and more in keeping with Walters and Parke's (1965) suggestion, that tactile exploration does not decrease with age. It is not possible, therefore, to argue that one hierarchical pattern replaces another in normal development, with an arrest of development in the case of the psychotic children. One suggestion which has been confirmed is the relatively short visual inspection time shown by the psychotic child. Our own work has a bearing on this issue.

Goldfarb (1956, 1961) showed that psychotic children did not differ from normals in their sensory thresholds for vision, audition and touch. He regards their failure to respond to stimuli appropriately as due to hypersensitivity or hyposensitivity. Comparing test response with re- sponse to visual and auditory signals in non-experimental settings, Gold- farb (1961) says: "specific receptor sensitivity is due less to reduced sensory threshold and more to emotional distress, primary or condi- tioned." He also thinks of sensory disturbances in psychotic children as the product of some failure of central integrative ability. There can be little doubt that by implicating sensory input functions, Goldfarb opened the way to a number of possibly fruitful hypotheses concerning learning difficulties and consequent social and behavioural disturbances in psychotic children. Goldfarb (1956) saw the perceptual pathology in psychotic children as central and possibly orectic in origin. But in suggesting a link between behaviour of patients with specific handicaps and that found in children with psychosis, he virtually stated an alternative hypothesis indicating biologically rather than emotionally determined behaviour.

Pollack (1958, 1960) and Pollack et al. (1957, 1958, 1959) explored brain dysfunction in schizophrenic children. In common with Goldfarb, Pollack uses the designation "schizophrenic", but describes, in fact, similar children to those referred to as autistic by others. The conclusions of his investigations are mainly concerned with physiological findings.

In one paper he examines oculomotor and vestibular responses in schizophrenic children (1958); in another (with Goldfarb, 1957) he notes the results of simultaneous stimulation of the face and hands of a schizophrenic child, and in a third (with Kreiger, 1958) he compares backward, brain damaged and schizophrenic children for their intelligence levels. He (1960) also makes a comparison of intelligence levels in schizophrenic children and adults. The conclusions of this work may be summarized by saying that Pollack finds that schizophrenic children make more numeration errors than normal in the face–hands test, that their intelligence levels are such as to suggest brain damage, that the diagnoses of childhood schizophrenia and mental defect overlap and that postural and vestibular reactions were abnormal in a large number of cases. This latter deviation was said to consist of involuntary head turning during optokinetic stimulation, inability to dissociate head movements and eye-movements, and minimal or absent post-rotational nystagmus.

This discussion covers one aspect of the experimental psychological work in the field. The work of Ferster (1961), Ferster and de Meyer (1961, 1962), Ferster (1964) and that of Lovaas et al. (1965) represent another group of experiments. This can be presented more simply because it is theoretically less ambitious, and the methodology in these studies is clear, although its mode of operation is open to discussion.

These authors use the operant conditioning of behaviour, as discussed by Skinner (1938) as a foundation for their approach to psychotic children. Ferster (1961) assumes that conditions in the child's early life have reinforced behaviour patterns which can be deconditioned by appropriate techniques. A basic assumption is that most forms of behaviour are available to manipulation, but that in the psychotic child the behaviour is not easily subject to social control. He concedes that there is some limitation of available responses, and that most of the children's performances are of a simple sort. Ferster speculates on the extent to which the interaction of parent and child can result in the reinforcement of abnormal behaviour in the child and aversive behaviour in the parent.

One of the problems about the conditioning of behaviour with operant techniques is that of widening the repertoire of the subject, and another is that of finding a stable reinforcer. A third is the gradual elimination of the reinforcer. Ferster and de Meyer (1962) elicited previously absent matching responses to visual material by immediate reward techniques, and so demonstrated some aspects of the latent behavioural repertoires of autistic children.

Lovaas *et al.* (1965) have used operant conditioning techniques as behaviour therapy. Lovaas' approach is to link reward as infallibly as possible with the behaviour to be maximized, to ensure acquisition under optimum drive and to determine the elimination of irrelevant behaviour as far as possible during training sessions. His use of attention-getting techniques and the elimination of irrelevant responses by electric shock and withholding of food has had some notable effects. Like Ferster, Lovaas draws attention to the failure of some children to connect primary (e.g. food rewards) and secondary (e.g. the smile of approval) reinforcements. Prompts are used to indicate the required movement or behaviour wanted from the child and such prompts are faded as the link between the behaviour and the reinforcement is strengthened. "Inappropriate" behaviours are concurrently extinguished by withholding all reinforcers or by physical punishment. Required behaviours are thus increased in frequency and brought under control. Lovaas (1966) observes that sympathetic treatment of the patient following irrelevant behaviour only increases its frequency.

Verbal behaviour has sometimes been induced in previously mute autistic children in a surprisingly short time by this technique. In fact, in one report (Lovaas, 1966), the time was so short that the reader might think that the technique, at least in this case, was forcing an existing potential rather than creating language *de novo*. Much of the work relies to some extent on a child's imitative propensities, and would vary accordingly in its absolute success or in the speed of its success.

Despite the practical success of the technique which is apparent in the number of cases successfully treated, Lovaas chooses to by-pass theoretical questions, although he is aware of the points which have a direct bearing on the practical value of the technique. For example, he is concerned with the possibility of generalizing a success from one therapist to another, from one laboratory to another, e.g. into the home, and from one item of behaviour to another. As yet, it seems as if each operant must be individually treated. Another important question is that of the spontaneous development of behaviour, initiation rather than imitation. This applies particularly to speech. Present reports clearly indicate the possibility of producing response words, phrases and sentences of some complexity, but less certainly demonstrate the spontaneous initiation of verbal demands and questions.

The whole of this area of investigation is distinct from the kind of experiments we will present below. Neither Ferster nor Lovaas show a great deal of interest in explanatory hypotheses, being concerned rather with educational techniques and their success. We, on the contrary, emphasize the role of the relevant psychological processes. It is not necessary to judge one approach as preferable to the other, but simply to note the difference. Others working in the field of behaviour therapy with autistic children, such as Breger (1965) deal with the problem of generalization of training by referring to Rimland's dictum that in early infantile autism there is a lack of ability to generalize. Perhaps the most theoretically interesting of these additional studies is that of Metz (1965) concerning conditioned generalized imitation. Metz conditioned the imitation of simple tasks and found an increase in generalized response over training periods. It is regrettable that his report does not define "generalized" more precisely and only uses two subjects.

A group of workers who have contributed to the study of autistic children by experiment and interpretation are Hutt and her collaborators. Their experiments are concerned with arousal as judged by EEG and other behavioural indicators, and with different types of social response under varying environmental conditions.

Hutt et al. (1964) propound a hypothesis in terms of a chronically high arousal level in the reticular system to account for autistic behaviour as described by Kanner. This high level of arousal is thought to account for flat desynchronized EEGs with much low voltage irregular activity, irrespective of whether eyes are opened or closed. Stereotypy could be decreased by reducing the complexity of the environment. This, the authors conclude, may be why autistic children attempt "to preserve sameness" and avoid novelty which would result in additional activation of the reticular system. The authors draw attention to the similarity of this kind of condition and adult schizophrenia, and infer from other work that chlorpromazine by reason of its effectiveness in adult schizophrenia and its action on the Ascending Reticular Activating System may be therapeutic with autistic children.

The same authors (Hutt et al., 1965) analysed both the behaviour and the EEG records of ten autistic children between the ages of 3 and 6 years.

In two cases behavioural and EEG studies were done simultaneously. Behaviour was studied by recording eye fixations, locomotion, object manipulation and gestures. Children were observed in four situations; firstly, in an empty waiting room, secondly with coloured blocks placed in the same room, thirdly in the same room with blocks and a female attendant, and finally, with the attendant involving the child in a game. Autistic children, unlike controls, showed few changes in mean number of fixations for the different situations and also many fewer fixations altogether were recorded. The same pattern of scores appeared when manipulatory activity was measured. Another finding was that in the normal group and in those autistic children who did not show stereo-typies, manipulations, gestures and locomotion declined as more items were introduced into the situation. This was not so for those with stereo-topy. Stereotypies were interpreted as a defence against overstimu-lation, although the validity of such an interpretation has not been established.

Hutt and Vaizey (1966) studied group density and its effect on the social behaviour of autistic children. The main effect of increasing density on autistic children was that they retreated to the corners and edges of the room and increased their contact with adults but not with children. The five autistic children in this study were aged between 3 and 8. An increase of group density meant putting either six or less, or seven to eleven, or more than twelve children together in a 27 by 17.5 foot play-ground. Time sampling of aggressive or destructive behaviour, or of social interactions or of withdrawal to the perimeter was scored. Control groups were brain injured ($N = 5$) or normal ($N = 5$).

Brain-damaged and normal children showed increased aggressive behaviour with increase in density, but autistic children did not. Normals showed fewer social contacts as density increased. In the same situation the brain injured showed more. Retreats to the perimeter increased in autistic children with increasing density, but the reverse (if anything) was seen in normals.

Another experiment, Hutt and Ounsted (1966) recorded the compara-tive visual inspection responses of normal and autistic children to different face masks mounted in an experimental room. Three human masks, happy, sad and blank, and two animal masks, monkey and dog, were displayed. Time spent on each, or time spent looking elsewhere in the room was measured for eight autistic and six non-autistic children who entered the room for a 10-minute period. The autistic children spent a far higher proportion of the total time recorded looking elsewhere, as compared with the controls. They naturally looked less at the displays under these circumstances. Hutt and Ounsted note that the autistic group looked significantly less than the normals at the two human masks "happy" and "sad", but not at "blank". Differences between the groups on the animal masks were in the same direction but were not significant.

The arousal theory advanced by these authors concerning observed behaviour, requires that the autistic child should see a waiting room as less "arousing" than a waiting room containing a box of bricks or a box of bricks and a person. In our own experiments concerning social response and EEG, results were obtained which differ from these. The reasons for the differences will be discussed in later chapters. Though interesting, the conclusions stated by Hutt and her colleagues often seem to go beyond the experimental evidence which has actually been obtained. One could also criticize the very small numbers of children used. The value of attempting to explain a large number of behavioural variables with a single unitary concept is questionable. In many such instances, other explanations may fit the data equally well, and as Broadbent (1967) has pointed out, theorizing only serves a useful purpose if the theory advanced is able to account for the facts better than any alternative theory.

SUMMARY

The study of childhood psychosis or autism since Kanner's (1943) early observations, has resulted in exploratory investigations in several fields of interest. In one the investigators are concerned with interpersonal relations, in another with perceptual or cognitive dysfunction, and in a third with possible genetic or physiological abnormalities. Other problems which have been considered have included descriptions of symptoms, terminology, prevalence, age of onset and outcome. Some agreement has been reached in delineating the syndrome, although in many ways there is still much unclarity. Poor or absent speech, mannerisms and repetitive behaviour, and apparently inappropriate responses to sensory stimulation, constitute the three most generally agreed behavioural manifestations of the disorder. Autism itself is less "durable" as a symptom, often declining with age. Prevalence at 4 per 10,000 seems to be a figure now reasonably well established, and age of onset between birth and 2 years is generally accepted. Male–female sex ratios of about 2.5 to 1 are commonly found. Prognosis is not encouraging, with 50 per cent still remaining in care at adolescence. Only 15 per cent enter the normal education system or make fair social adjustments. Improvement, where it occurs, is mainly in those of IQs above 60 points.

Theories propounded are not necessarily mutually exclusive. One which has interested us is that of Anthony (1962) with its basis in Piaget's ideas of stages in child development. The concept of failure of development at a particular point before the recognition of object constancy and the difficulty of establishing a coherent concept structure without language would help to explain some aspects of autistic behaviour.

Psychological theories are of several kinds. The first explains autism as a failure to co-ordinate input and memory, and is rather similar to Anthony's view. This theory of the failure to develop "abstraction" was used originally by Scheerer et al. to explain the idiot savant but has been adapted by Rimland (1964) to account for some aspects of autism, e.g. the tendency to arrange or order the external world, and the literalness or concreteness of verbal interpretation. The second view, most prominently expounded by Ferster (1961), and Lovaas (1966), sees learning deficits or faulty learning as the basis of the aberrant behaviour, and attempts to correct and recondition responses. It is an environmentalist theory. The third type of theory is that of Hutt et al., who regard peculiarities of response in autistic children as a defence mechanism against over-arousal from too intense stimulation. A condition of hyperarousal probably depending on a disturbance of the reticular formation is posited. Another view, held by Wing, is that autistic children suffer from multiple perceptual deficits. Goldfarb and Schopler place emphasis on the autistic child's preoccupation with proximal receptor stimulation.

THE PRESENT STUDY: THE SELECTION OF SUBJECTS

As was noted in the previous discussion, the selection of subjects presents some problems. Any method of selection is open to objections and the best that can be done at present is to make a precise statement of the criteria used. This book describes psychological experiments with autistic children and normal and subnormal controls. The use of subnormal controls may need some justification. As most autistic children function at a severely subnormal level, it is possible that much of their behaviour could be explained on the basis of low intelligence. Thus an attempt to control for intellectual level would enable us to attribute any behaviour which distinguished autistic children from mental defectives specifically to autism or childhood psychosis. Hyperkinesis and stereotyped behaviour, for example, often regarded as characteristic of autism, have also been observed to occur in the severely subnormal, e.g. Earl (1934), Berkson and Davenport (1962). While it is relatively easy to distinguish autistic and normal children, the distinction between autism and subnormality may be more difficult and will depend on detailed analysis of experimental results.

The samples of autistic children used in the studies to be described have been selected on the basis of psychiatric diagnosis. The children taking part in our experiments were firstly a large, somewhat heterogeneous group of seventy-seven subjects, and a second, more homogeneous group of twenty-seven out of those seventy-seven children, who form the core of our experimental subjects. We think that this group can justifiably be called autistic, in the sense in which the term has been defined by Wing (1966) or Rutter (1967). While each member of the large sample took part in at least one of the experiments, the children from the latter, smaller group participated in most of the studies which will be reported. The children of this group all lived at home and attended a special school. The remaining fifty children lived in mental deficiency institutions or in other special units.

Large Sample

These subjects, aged between 6 and 16 years, were selected according to two criteria. The first of these was a psychiatric diagnosis of infantile autism or childhood psychosis. The names of the children so diagnosed were then given to two further people who knew the children well, i.e. nurses or teachers. These observers were also given a check-list of the nine diagnostic points developed by Creak *et al.* (1961) and were asked to specify which of these, if any, applied to any particular child. Only those children who were described as showing at least four of these behavioural characteristics were included in the sample. From the children thus selected, we excluded all those with obvious severe sensory or motor impairments, all those who functioned at an idiot level and were therefore unable to participate in the experiments, and all those cases in which a definite diagnosis additional to psychosis, such as mongolism or phenylketonuria, had been made. An investigation of the records of remaining subjects was made from which information about prenatal, natal and postnatal histories was recorded. Information about the families and results of neurological investigations were also collected. Table 1 summarizes this information. The same data from two control groups of subnormal mongol and non-mongol children was also collected.

TABLE 1. SUMMARY TABLE OF PATHOLOGICAL DATA
(Large Sample (Percentage))

	Psychotic (N = 77)	SSN (N = 49)	Mongols (N = 20)	SSN+ Mongols (N = 69)
Premature	12	16	10	14
Difficult and prolonged birth	16	8	0	6
Low intelligence in one or both parents	3	27	5	20
Mental illness or subnormality in sibs	1	20	10	17
Strabismus	13	18	10	16
Seizures	19	22	5	17
No speech	51	4	10	6

The items which most clearly differentiate the groups are absence of speech, and low intellectual status of parents. The first is present to a far greater extent in the psychotic group than in either of the subnormal ones. The second is marked in the non-mongol subnormal group, and minimal in the mongols and in the psychotics. Sibs in the psychotic group are not affected, but are frequently mentally subnormal or mentally ill for the non-mongols, and also, though to a lesser extent, for the mongols. Prematurity is relatively frequent for all groups.

The somewhat more frequent reports of prolonged or difficult birth in the psychotic groups is not statistically different from that for the SSN. As most of this information was obtained from case records and was based on retrospective reporting, the validity and reliability of the data is limited.

Small Sample

Twenty-seven out of the sample of seventy-seven children were included in a detailed investigation by Wing (1967). They were compared with mongol, aphasic and deaf-blind children. The autistic children, who were all so diagnosed, attended a special school and lived at home. There were twenty boys and seven girls, and twenty children were first-born. Onset at birth or during the first 20 months of life was observed in all. The clinical information is summarized in Table 2.

TABLE 2. SUMMARY TABLE OF PATHOLOGICAL DATA:
SMALL SAMPLE OF AUTISTIC CHILDREN
(N = 27)

Early onset	27
Males	20
First-born	20
Pregnancy complications	12
Birth complications	11
Seizures	2
Mental abnormality in family	0
"Soft" neurological signs	4

A detailed questionnaire was completed by the parents of the autistic and the control children.

The questionnaire was based on behaviour that is held to be characteristic of early infantile autism. The ratings were made (retrospectively) for the age period 2–5 years and the 172 items concerned with this period of life were grouped into seventeen categories, namely:

Group A. Auditory perception and speech.

Abnormalities in:
1. Response to sound.
2. Comprehension of speech.
3. Use of speech.

Group B. Motor control.

Abnormalities in:
4. Pronunciation and voice control.
5. Performing other skilled movements (apraxias).

Group C. Visual perception and related functions.

Abnormalities in:
6. Response to visual stimuli.
7. Use and understanding of gesture.
8. Use of proximal senses.
9. Bodily movements.

Group D. Behaviour problems.

Abnormalities in:
10. Social relationships.
11. Resistance to change.
12. Mood.
13. Lack of constructive play.
14. Socially embarrassing behaviour.

Group E. Deficits in non-verbal skills and interests.

15. Musical ability.
16. Manipulative ability.
17. Spatial ability.

According to Wing (1967), the autistic children all had high (i.e. abnormal) scores on all the categories, apart from non-verbal skills, in which they resembled the normal children. The normal children had low scores on all categories. Mongol children in general had low scores apart from their difficulties in pronunciation, and their marked lack of non-verbal skills.

Receptive aphasic children closely resembled autistic children in their problems with auditory perception, speech and pronunciation, but they had no difficulties with skilled movements or with visual perception.

Expressive aphasic children had problems of pronunciation and difficulties in skilled movements.

The partially deaf–partially blind group had almost the same scores as the autistic children on all the basic handicaps (groups A, B and C) and their behaviour problems (D) were near those of the autistic children. They could not be rated on use of speech, pronunciation or performance of skilled movements (apraxias) because of the severity of their handicaps. Wing's conclusions from the analysis of the questionnaires were:

(a) autistic children appeared to have multiple handicaps, combining several kinds of problems each of which may occur alone in other syndromes;

(b) the more handicaps a child has, the more severe and widespread his secondary behaviour problems.

The intellectual level of this sample ranged from normal to severely subnormal. (Bartak, to be published.) Mean IQ on the Merrill–Palmer Performance scales was 56, ranging from 23 to 99. Two children scored between 80 and 100, eight between 60 and 79, twelve between 40 and 59 and five between 20 and 39. All children proved to be testable, an observation confirming that of Rutter (1966). On a verbal scale (Peabody Picture Vocabulary), the mean mental age was 4–0 years, compared with a mean of 5–6 years on the performance scale. Two children had a verbal mental age above 10 years, which in both cases was considerably higher than their performance MA. If these children are excluded from the calculation, the mean verbal mental age of the group is 3 years 3 months. Chronological ages ranged from 6 years 4 months, to 15 years 3 months, mean 10 years 4 months. All these autistic children had learning difficulties and lacked social skills. Though they tended to be poor in forming relationships, except through physical contact, not all were aloof or distant in manner at the time the investigations were carried out. However, all were reported to have been withdrawn and unsociable at some stage of their development. After a short initial period of acquaintance, little difficulty was found in establishing contact and gaining the children's co-operation.

CHAPTER 2

PERCEPTION AND
PERCEPTUAL DEFICITS

SENSORY IMPAIRMENT IN AUTISTIC CHILDREN

It is understandable that educators who thought that information about the outside world comes to us through our senses, have long held the view that an inability to "make sense" of the world may be due to an inability to receive or organize the incoming sense data. "Sense training", or the benefit of a varied and systematic acquaintance with sensory attributes of objects and events, was used by Itard (1801) with the "wild boy of Aveyron". Itard's account may well be the first case history of an autistic child. He describes how the boy, who was found living naked in the woods, showed no sign of affection for anyone, and how he seemed to be unable to use his eyes and ears adequately. He led people by the hand to demonstrate to them what he wanted, like autistic children, and was unable to learn to play with toys. He resisted change, and despite supposed sensory unresponsiveness, had an excellent memory for the position of objects in the room, which he rigidly maintained. He would explore objects by touching and smelling them, and seemed insensitive to heat and cold. Itard's attempts at sense training had only limited success. The child never learned to speak, but eventually he was able to follow some written instructions, and his social behaviour improved.

Abnormal responses to sensory stimuli are one of the central features in the behaviour of autistic children. This may take the form of under- or over-reacting to stimulation, and sometimes these two forms of response are found in the same child. The child may also use "inappropriate" senses if confronted with various objects and situations. This behaviour is so marked that some investigators have tended to regard autism as the consequence of multiple sensory handicap. There are, indeed, striking

24

parallels between autistic children and those deprived of one or more senses, like the blind or the deaf. As has already been mentioned, one of the more recent studies was carried out by Wing (1967) who compared several groups of children with each other. The groups included autistic children, children who were partly blind and deaf, mongols, children with expressive and receptive aphasia, and normal children. Abnormal responses to auditory as well as visual stimuli, and a preference for the use of the proximal senses, was significantly more marked in the autistic than in the normal or mongol groups. The group which resembled autistic children most in their sensory response patterns was the partially deaf-blind group. These children also showed the same amount of abnormal motility patterns as the autistic ones, i.e. jumping, spinning, or general hyperactivity.

Similarities in the behaviour of blind and autistic children have been noted frequently. Keeler (1958) and Blank (1959) have found behaviour and mannerisms which strongly resemble those found in autism. In Russia, Kistiakorskaia (1965) found that in children with retarded visual responses there was also a lack of emotional and social responsiveness. Visual retardation in these children was defined as a lack of visual convergence, and extended fixation of near objects. Walters and Parke (1965) have reviewed a large number of studies which link social responsiveness in infants to the role played by the distance receptors for vision and hearing.

Many workers have stated that autistic children use proximal as much or more than distance senses for exploring the environment (Goldfarb, 1961), Rimland (1964) and Wing (1966). They tend to touch, smell, lick, bang and shake things, the latter often apparently for the resulting vibrations rather than for sounds. However, there are also many observations of lack of response to heat, cold and pain, so that a hypothesis for more sensitive proximal receptor changes is an oversimplification. Rutter (1966) found ten autistic children in his sample of fifty-seven, with an absence, or relative absence of responses to painful stimulation, though four subnormal children behaved in a similar manner. In regard to distance receptors, auditory imperception is the most frequently reported sensory anomaly in autism. Goldfarb (1961), Anthony (1958a, 1958b) and Rutter (1966) found lack of stable responses to sudden noises, as well as strong reactions to very soft noises, frequently in the same child.

Hermelin and O'Connor (1968), investigating EEG responses to light and sound in autistic, normal and mongol children, found no group differences in orienting responses to light, but there was an indication that a continuous noise was more arousing for the autistic children than for the other groups. This investigation will be discussed in more detail further on. However, in the light of work such as Furth's (1964) with the deaf, there seems little justification for attributing the intellectual impairment found in the majority of autistic children only to their lack of appreciation of auditory stimuli. In this connection Piaget (1965) has pointed out that the blind may be more seriously retarded in conceptual operations than the deaf.

Several factors may contribute to the apparently abnormal responses of autistic children to sensory stimuli. Amongst them are the possible role of interest and motivation, the level of arousal of the subject, the connection between low verbal ability and perceptual impairment, and the interpretation and integration of information from different sensory systems. In the present chapter, the first points will be dealt with only briefly, and are more adequately discussed in appropriate chapters, while the last question will concern us in some detail.

It is frequently asked whether the performance of autistic children on cognitive tests gives a true indication of their capacity, or whether it reflects the child's lack of interest in the material and the tasks. Somewhat related are problems of the interpretation of the results of experiments using conditioned responses as measures of perceptual or intellectual ability, such as in discrimination learning. Performances at such tasks may remain at chance level either because the child cannot discriminate between the stimuli, or because he is content with relatively infrequent reinforcement, or because, though able to appreciate differences in the display stimuli, he is unable to link a consistent response with one of these stimuli. Many of these problems could be overcome by applying methods such as those used by investigators concerned with infant behaviour e.g. Lipsitt (1963) and Bower (1965, 1966). These measure and reinforce orienting responses to a single stimulus, and are not dependent on operative discrimination response. In evaluating the role of reinforcement, associative processes and response factors, Wohlwill (1966) concludes that these variables often affect perceptual judgements rather than the perceptual processes on which they are based. A similar argument could be put forward to account for the effects of words on performance in perceptual tasks. Interpretations such as those of Luria (1961), O'Connor and Hermelin (1959) and Kendler *et al.* (1966), that the introduction of words directly affects perception of the named stimuli, may not be fully justified and may need qualifications, as has been shown by Bryant (1965, 1967a and 1967b). Verbal labels may only focus attention on the discriminable aspects of stimuli, or act as mediators on perceptual judgements and decisions.

VISUAL DISCRIMINATION

Visual discrimination and discrimination learning capacity can only be judged by observing behaviour. Thus whatever may be happening at any one level of the discrimination process has to be inferred from overt performance on a task. For this reason the analysis of discrimination as a function has generally been based on operant behaviour.

One can assume that the foundation of response behaviour is an initial orientation towards sensory input and a judgement concerning the nature of this input, which involves categorizing or coding. Experiments have indicated that some animals noted accidental aspects of a stimulus display while ostensibly only attending to the critical one. Hull (1945) observed that different aspects of a display had a greater or lesser likelihood of making an impact on a subject according to its species, and Spence (1945) drew attention to the difference between the relevant stimulus aspects of a display as distinct from the appropriate perceptual responses. Mackintosh (1965) summarizes evidence for the failure or ability of animals to notice more than one perceptual cue at a time. He concludes that results point to a modified non-continuity theory of discrimination, according to which certain perceptual dimensions may have a species determined likelihood to be observed more readily than others. This may also apply to different chronological or mental ages in children.

However, usually stimuli are not observed according to one single dimension only. Bryant (1965) found that subnormal children could transfer sorting behaviour on the basis of the previously relevant as well as the irrelevant stimulus dimensions. There was no difference in transfer performance in his experiments, indicating that responding to a relevant stimulus dimension was as readily transferred as not responding to an irrelevant one. The relative difficulty of discrimination along different visual dimensions has been investigated by Zeaman et al. (1958) for subnormals, and by Hermelin and O'Connor (1965) for autistic children. Problems of orientation have been examined by Ghent (1961) and by Rudel and Teuber (1963). While children readily distinguished between shapes which appeared as "upside-down" or "right-side up", and also took focal points into account, they found left–right discriminations, and those concerned with the direction of lines much more difficult.

Broadbent (1958) in emphasizing the selectivity of sensory input, puts forward an attentional model in which "filters" may be set in such a way that certain sensory channels or certain stimulus dimensions are more readily perceived than others. The selection of such filters is treated by Sutherland and Mackintosh (Mackintosh, 1965) in terms of different sensory analysers which can be "switched in", to deal successively rather than simultaneously with various stimulus dimensions. The question is which variables affect the selection of a particular dimension, and which dimensions are dominant at any one stage of development or in any one condition of deviation from normal development.

There are, broadly speaking, two main sets of theories to account for perceptual operations. One stresses the role of activity and of feedback from motor movements, including those from the eyes. The main exponents of such a view have been Hebb (1949), Piaget (1952), Zaporozhets (1961) and Held (1961). Emphasis on the analysis of perceptual input has been stressed by Sutherland (1964) who proposed a discrimination model which was originally based on neural counting of the vertical and horizontal extent of shapes. Later the suggestion has been in terms of differential pairing of cortical striate cells as a result of the projection of differently orientated retinal receptive fields. Thus while one theory lays stress on perceptual activity, the other is mainly concerned with perceptual analyses. Other relevant aspects for discrimination are the role of mediational processes and language, which has concerned Luria (1961) and Kendler and Kendler (1966). There certainly seems to be a tendency for dominance of the auditory–vocal systems over the visual, when the material is verbal. Conrad (1964) has demonstrated that auditory confusion errors occur even in visually presented material, and Conrad and Rush (1965) have shown that there was an absence of this kind of error in the deaf. Gibson et al. (1962) found fewer errors in recognizing tachitoscopically exposed pronounceable nonsense words than unpronounceable ones, and Pick *et al.* (1966) repeated these findings with blind subjects in the perception of braille. However, the relative dominance of the auditory over the visual and tactile systems is perhaps not too surprising when verbal material is involved, and facilitating effects as well as acoustic confusion may occur at the output rather than the input stages. At present, most discrimination models are more logically satisfying than comprehensive or adequate, but the problem is clearly complex. A complete model of discrimination in humans must involve alerting, orientation, selection, resolution, matching to category or to sample, memory, verbal nomination or mediation, manipulation of stimulus and ultimate operant response. Though such a model has not always been in our minds in planning experiments with autistic children, ultimately deviations from the normal development in terms of such a model must be considered.

In the following experiments we have been concerned with visual, auditory, tactile and kinesthetic perception, and with their interrelationship. We investigated intra as well as interdimensional patterns, and attempted to link the perceptual impairments found in the autistic children to other aspects of the syndrome.

Visual Discrimination Experiments with Autistic Children

In the first experiment to be described (O'Connor and Hermelin, 1967a), we were concerned with the question of whether or not autistic children were able to perceive differences between various kinds of visual stimuli. As a measure of discrimination, we used visual inspection time for two simultaneously presented displays. Similar techniques have been used to investigate perceptual development in infants.

Each child was tested individually while sitting at a table with a viewing box in front of him. The box had an opening in the front through which the subject could put his head and look inside. A flap, hinged to the roof of the box, could be raised to permit the subject to see the displays. These consisted of two cards, $2\frac{1}{2}$ by $2\frac{1}{2}$ inches, mounted vertically in slots at an angle of 35° either side of the midline. These cards, which were 15 inches from the subject's eyes, were illuminated by lights. Otherwise the inside of the box, painted a uniform matt black, was in shadow.

Opposite the subject's viewing aperture was a small peep-hole, which allowed the experimenter to observe the subject's eye movements. A three-way switch connected to a pen recorder enabled the experimenter to record at any time the direction in which the subject was looking, i.e. at the left or the right display card, or elsewhere in the box. A quantified determination of such eye movements in the presence of two visual stimuli could be held to show that if one were looked at longer than the other, the two were presumably distinguishable for the viewer. As no learning was involved in this procedure, verbal instructions were unnecessary, and speaking as well as non-speaking children could be used. Three groups of twenty-eight children, one normal, one subnormal, and one autistic group took part. They were matched for their performance on the Seguin formboard, which corresponded to mental ages of 6–0, 6–0 and 5–3 respectively. Mean chronological ages were 5–4 for normals, 14.4 for the subnormals and 10–9 for the autistic children. The normal children were in a day nursery in London, the severely subnormals lived in an institution, and the autistic children either lived in hospital or at home while attending special schools. Half of the autistic group had no speech.

In order to conclude that selective fixation of one of the two displays implied a discrimination ability on the part of the viewer, it was, of course, necessary to establish that identical stimuli would be fixated for an equal amount of time, irrespective of whether they were on the right or left side of the display. Thus one pair of stimuli were two plain white cards. The other pairs were similar to those used by Fantz (1965). They were one large and one small blue card, a red versus a black card, one black card with a white corner, together with a white card with a black corner, a black and white striped card versus a grey one of the same overall brightness, and a black circle, and parts of the circle cut up and rearranged randomly. Finally, there was a photograph of a human face, together with the same photograph cut up and rearranged at random. Thus the dimensions to be investigated were: (a) identity, (b) size, (c) colour, (d) brightness, (e) pattern, (f) complexity and (g) meaningfulness. The displays are illustrated in Fig. 1. The order of presentation of each of these seven pairs was randomized between subjects, as was the presentation of any one of a pair of cards on either the right or left side. Sweets were given between presentation, as rewards for the children's continued co-opera-

FIG. 1. Material for fixation time experiment.

tion. However, little difficulty was experienced in maintaining their involvement with the apparatus if not with each display.

Subjects were first shown the display box and the experimenter demonstrated how to look into it by putting his head through the opening. The child was then told to look into the box himself. When he had placed his head inside, the flap was raised, revealing the lit-up display cards for a period of 30 seconds. Scores were obtained from the paper records, in which the direction of the fixation had been recorded. There were three scores within each 30-second period, two which recorded time spent looking at one or the other of the two display cards, and the third giving the amount of time which the subject spent not looking at either stimulus, but gazing around the box. A first analysis of variance showed that for all groups the time of such "non-directed gazing" increased within each 30-second period, and correspondingly the time spent looking at the stimulus cards decreased. There was no interaction in this analysis, demonstrating that adaptation took place at about the same rate for all three groups. The analysis of the data also revealed that the autistic children had significantly lower fixation scores, and higher undirected gaze scores than the other two groups. Thus, when presented with two lit-up stimulus cards in an otherwise dark and featureless surround, the autistic children spent less time looking at these cards and more time gazing around the dark interior of the box than the other subjects. This effect was independent of the pair of cards presented.

A comparison of the amount of time the subjects spend looking at any of the seven pairs of cards (as distinct from the time spent looking at one member of a pair) showed that the two identical white cards were looked at for the shortest time. The two cards showing the photographs, i.e. a face, and the same photograph cut up and randomly reassembled, were examined for a significantly longer period than any other pair. Pairs of cards showing colours, sizes and shapes were looked at for an intermediate amount of time, in that order. As far as a comparison within pairs was concerned, the red card was looked at for longer than the black one, the striped for longer than the grey, and the face for longer than the randomly assembled parts. These were the only significant differences, and they were true for all groups. No difference in fixation time was found for the two identical white cards, the large versus the small, or the brighter versus the darker member of a stimulus pair, or the circle versus the randomly arranged parts of the circle. Thus, the only variable in this study in which the autistic children differed from normals and subnormals, was that they spent less time examining the stimuli and more time in gazing round the box. When they did look at the display cards, the relative distribution of time spent looking was the same as that of the other children in a between-pairs as well as in a within-pairs comparison.

If the time spent looking at one particular card is measured, the resultant score may be derived in two ways. Suppose that card A was looked at for 5 seconds out of a total 10-second period. This could mean either that the subject looked continuously for 5 seconds at the card, and the rest of time somewhere else, or that he gave several repeated briefer glances, amounting altogether to 5 seconds. We compared the number of such eye movements from one display to the other between the groups. This comparison showed that the normals gave frequent brief glances at the display cards, whereas the subnormal and autistic children achieved their inspection scores by more uninterrupted fixations. The comparison between the normal and subnormal children is particularly interesting, as their overall inspection time of the display cards was not statistically different. But whereas the normals look from one member of a pair of cards to the other and back again, the subnormals look first at one, then at the other for longer periods in each case, and make few repeated rapid comparisons. This difference in inspecting two stimuli may possibly be related to problems in visual discrimination learning found in the subnormal. If, on the other hand, one compares the subnormal with the autistic children, one finds that both make an equal number of comparisons. But the relatively uninterrupted fixation of one stimulus card followed by fixation of the other is significantly shorter in the autistic than in the subnormal children. Thus not only do the autistic children make fewer comparisons between two stimuli than normals, they also look at each of them for a briefer time period than the subnormals. Figure 2 shows that autistic children make the same number of eye movements as the subnormals, but fixate the displays for a shorter time. One can infer from this that their eye movements are from figure to background, rather than from one figure to the other.

Clinical observation indicates that one of the most characteristic features in the behaviour of many children diagnosed as autistic is their apparent imperception of visual as well as auditory and other sensory stimuli, in the absence of any observable sensory defect. A more detailed psychological examination reveals that the relationship between perception and overt response behaviour is a complex one. The eye movement experiment gave an indication, that as fixation time between red and black, stripes and grey, and face versus non-face differed, these stimuli seem to be perceived as different. However, the argument is not reversible. It is true that identical cards were fixated for an identical amount of time,

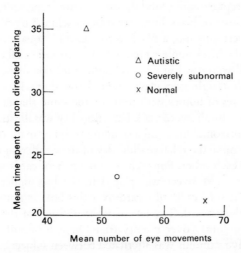

FIG. 2. Group means of eye movements and non-directed gazing.

but so were some non-identical stimulus pairs, and it does not follow that differences between them were not perceived.

The eye movement experiment did not require the subjects to make an operant discrimination response. If such a response had been required, different results might have been obtained, i.e. there may be a difference between discrimination capacity and discrimination learning. The next experiment was planned to investigate this (Hermelin and O'Connor, 1965). Thirty-six children acted as subjects. Twenty-four of these had been diagnosed as autistic, using the Creak criteria as well as supplementary psychiatric diagnosis. Twelve additional children were selected as being free of autistic symptoms. They were all severely subnormal. The subjects were matched for chronological age, and for their performance on the Seguin formboard. They were also tested on the Peabody Picture Vocabulary, and the autistic subjects were divided into two subgroups of twelve, with those who obtained a verbal mental age below 2–6 years in one group, and those who scored above that in the other. The relevant data is given in Table 3. Visual discrimination of four different dimensions was investigated: brightness, size, shape and directionality. For each of these dimensions two examples were used: one which presented the variables in a representative, and the other in non-representative form. The material consisted of black line drawings on white 3 by 5 inch cards. For brightness discrimination, a black versus a white square or the drawings of a white and a black apple were used. A large and small circle, and large and small ball were used in size discrimination. For shape discrimination a triangle with straight sides was presented, together with one with curved sides, or pictures of houses with roofs of the same shapes as in the non-representative stimuli, were used. Directionality was illustrated by a vertical versus a horizontal line, and a standing or lying man. No attempt was made to determine the relative difficulty of these different discriminations in relation to each other. For each session a pair of cards was placed over cardboard boxes. A sweet was placed in the box under the "correct" card, and if the subject lifted a card over this box or pointed towards it, he obtained the reward. The left or right position of the rewarded box was varied randomly over twenty trials. Which one of a pair of cards was the positive stimulus was alternated between subjects. Each child was tested individually on all eight tasks. Representative or non-representative material was given first or second to alternate subjects, and the order of presenting the tasks representing the four dimensions was varied according to a 4 by 4 Latin square. An analysis of variance of the number of correct choices under each condition showed that the main effects of groups and dimensions were both highly significant. There was also a significant groups by dimensions interaction. This demonstrated that while all dimensions were equally easily discriminated by the normal children, the speaking autistics found shape and direction significantly more difficult than brightness or size. The non-speaking autistic children gave responses on a chance level on all tasks. There was no difference in results according to whether the material was presented in representational or non-representational form.

TABLE 3. DISCRIMINATION EXPERIMENT

(Mean chronological and mental ages (in years and months) for speaking and non-speaking autistic children)

Group	N	Chronological age		Seguin mental age		Peabody mental age	
		Mean	Range	Mean	Range	Mean	Range
Speakers	10	11–2	9–7 to 14–6	5–1	4–7 to 8–2	3–10	2–10 to 6–2
Non-speakers	10	10–9	7–2 to 14–6	6–1	3–1 to 12–0	1–11	1–8 to 2–4
Subnormal controls	10	10–5	8–5 to 13–6	5–10	4–0 to 13–6	4–2	2–4 to 6–1

In the eye movement study, no difference was found in fixating a small versus a large, or a darker versus a brighter card. However, as the present results show, it would have been unjustified to infer from this that these stimuli were perceived as identical, because in the present experiment, at least some of the children discriminated between them. As there was a difference between speaking and non-speaking autistic children in discrimination learning performance, one could ask whether the equal level of perceptual motor development or the differing verbal development determined visual discrimination learning. It could be held that while some aspects of visual discrimination are directly associated with mediating processes, others are not. Hebb (1949), for instance, has argued that pattern perception is more dependent on experience and learning than perception of brightness or size. Along these latter dimensions there is, on the whole, little difference in discrimination ability between higher and lower mammals. Hebb argued that this implied a difference in the mechanisms concerned between, for instance, size and form discrimination.

In our next experiment (Hermelin and O'Connor, 1965), we were concerned to examine the capacity for visual discrimination of directionality in speaking and non-speaking autistic children. The subjects were ten speaking, ten non-speaking autistic children aged between 9 and 14 years and ten matched subnormal controls. Chronological and mental ages are those in Table 3.

The autistic children, in addition to psychiatric diagnosis, were tested on the nine Creak criteria (Creak *et al.* 1961), and only those who showed at least four of the listed symptoms were included. Statistical analysis showed that the groups were equal in term of chronological and performance mental age, but that the non-speaking autistic children scored significantly lower on the verbal comprehension test than the other two groups. Three tasks had to be learned in succession. In the first, one of two upturned white cardboard boxes contained a sweet, which the child could obtain by lifting the correct box. While one box stood on the table, the other to the right or left of it stood on a 12-inch stand, so that one box was on a higher plane than the other. For alternate subjects the higher or lower placed box was correct. Ten errorless responses were taken as an indication that the task had been learned. Analyses of the results showed that the number of trials needed to reach this criterion was statistically the same for all three groups. This part of the experiment will be discussed further on. For the next task, a black arrow was painted on one of the boxes, whereas the surface of the other remained blank. Both boxes were now presented on the table at the same level, and for those for whom the upper box had been the correct one in the previous task, the arrow on the correct box pointed upwards. Conversely, those who had to select the lower box in task (A) were now required to select the box with the arrow pointing downwards. The left and right position of the correct box was randomly varied from trial to trial. In this second task, the difference between the speaking psychotic children and the normals was statistically non-significant. However, the non-speaking autistic children needed significantly more trials than the other groups to learn to select the box with the arrow, and some of them could not learn this discrimination task.

In the last task in this series, the two boxes each had a black arrow painted on them, on one box the arrow pointed vertically upwards, and on the other vertically downwards. Alternate children had to learn to lift one or the other box consistently to obtain the reward. Again, the difference between subnormal and speaking autistic children was not significant, but the difference between the non-speaking autistic group and the others was very marked and statistically highly significant. These results can be expressed in terms of the number of children who were successful in learning the tasks, as well as in terms of number of trials needed to learn. Thus all subjects learned the first task. In the second task all the subnormals and nine of the speaking autistic children learned, as well as six of the ten non-speaking children. In the last task, one subnormal child, three speaking autistic and all ten non-speaking autistic children were unsuccessful over sixty trials.

It is necessary to account for the fact that non-speaking autistic children, who obtained a mean mental age level of 5 years on a perceptual motor test were unable to learn to discriminate an upward from a downward pointing arrow in 60 trials. Rudel and Teuber (1963) found that normal three-year-olds readily learned a "right side up versus an upside down" discriminations ($\sqcap$ versus $\sqcup$). On the other hand, three- and four-year-olds were unable to distinguish between two oblique lines ($/$ versus $\setminus$). Even from amongst 8-year-old children, five out of seventeen failed to learn this task. The distinguishing aspects in our experiment, included differently slanted lines in the arrowheads ($\uparrow$ versus $\downarrow$). However, the arrowheads were placed at different points on the boxes, i.e. the upward pointing at the top and the downward near the bottom, and the focal points of the figures were presumably at different positions. Nevertheless, the discrimination seems to have been a difficult one. Though the inability of the non-speaking children to learn the task is associated with absence of speech, there need not be a causal connection. The inability to discriminate as well as the inability to name the stimuli may both be due to a third factor, such as amount of cortical dysfunction, and though the children were matched on mental age levels for the Seguin formboard, other aspects of mental functioning may have been relevant.

Over and Over (1967) point out that experimental results such as those by Rudel and Teuber (1963) in which young children were found to have difficulties in discriminating between oblique lines, may not be due to poor discrimination ability. Rather, the subjects may be unable to remember from trial to trial the spatial properties which define the shape associated with reinforcement. Over and Over found that many young children who were unable to discriminate between mirror image obliques when tested by discrimination learning techniques, were readily able to make such distinctions when two stimuli were simultaneously presented and had to be judged as "the same" or "different". The investigators concluded that deficiencies in the system by which spatial information is remembered, rather than in the input, coding, and analysing mechanisms in the visual system might be implicated. Similar mechanisms may account for the present results.

SENSORY DOMINANCE AND SENSORY INTEGRATION

The concept of sensory dominance, which differs between species and changes within a species during the course of development was put forward in the nineteenth century by Abbott (1882) who found that the frog cannot inhibit a visually determined response, despite the gradual destruction of the responding organ. He had a frog strike at a fly impaled on a stake. This lacerated the frog's tongue, but did not prevent it striking again. On the other hand, the frog will learn to adapt, if the feedback is directed to the taste instead of to the pain receptors. As these experiments were concerned with afferent receptors in the frog's tongue, it remains to be demonstrated whether or not pain receptors exist there. Pavlov (1927) demonstrated that with dogs a tone was dominant compared with a light in determining response behaviour, and contact with a cold object overshadowed tactual stimulation of the skin. Kupalow and Gantt (1928) found that a bright light or a cold stimulus would override a soft sound, and Rickman (1928) showed that while touch took precedence over a soft tone, it was overshadowed by a loud one. Zachiniaera (1950) carried out experiments in which dogs were presented simultaneously with light and sound. They responded to the sound, even if this response had previously been reinforced with bread, while responding to light had been reinforced with meat, which the dogs greatly preferred. Bernhaut *et al.* (1953) showed in their classical experiment that the most widespread and intense cortical arousal pattern in anaesthetized cats and monkeys was evoked by pain, followed by proprioceptive, auditory and finally by visual stimuli. On the other hand, certain fish and birds are more responsive to visual than to auditory stimulation (Vedanev and Karmanova, 1958). In regard to human development, the theory that touch teaches vision has been put forward by Zinchenko *et al.* (1959) and earlier by Renshaw (1930) and Renshaw and Wherry (1931). In neonates, somesthetic stimuli are most effective in eliciting non-specific cortical EEG responses, auditory stimuli next and visual stimuli least effective (Ellingson, 1960), Bronstein *et al.* (1958) found that orientation responses in infants indicated by an interruption of sucking, was most frequently aroused by auditory stimuli, followed by visual, vibratory, olfactory, tactile and thermal stimulation. The philosopher Berkeley suggested in 1709 that the infant explores "objects" mainly by moving towards and away from them and touching them, and it was through this that he discovered that all "objects" are three-dimensional, and have certain shapes and sizes, as well as orientation and location in space. A similar view of sensory development has been taken by Zaporozhets (1961) who quoted experimental results in which 3- to 4-year-old children needed manipulation of shapes in order to discriminate between them, while visual exploration alone was sufficient for older children. However, the experiments of Lipsitt (1963) and Bower (1966) on visual orientation in infants, and those by Birch *et al.* (1966) and Papousek (1967) on how one-day-old infants consistently orient towards auditory stimuli, clearly indicate that visual and auditory signals elicit responses soon after birth. Pick *et al.* (1967) reviewing the results from experiments on perceptual integration in children, conclude that the evidence indicates that visual perception approaches maturity earlier than tactual. The evidence for this conclusion includes the earlier development of visual discrimination as compared with tactual, and the dominance of visual information over tactual in sensory conflict situations. Apart from the studies already mentioned, Kershenson (1964) and Brennen *et al.* (1966) have shown that very young infants are able to make fine visual shape discrimination, and Graham *et al.* (1956) have found that neonates are able to track moving light. Specific evoked EEG responses to light in the newborn have been first recorded by Ellingson (1957). There are thus clear behavioural and physiological indicators of orientation towards distance receptor stimulation from birth onwards. It is possible, however, that though some thetic stimuli may be at first the most arousing, discriminations along the visual dimension are made earlier than along the tactual, and that arousal value and discrimination ability are not necessarily correlated.

An experiment by Benner and Cashdan (1967) with older children gave results which suggested that it was not tactile exploration which aided visual perception, but additional activity. In this experiment, not only the shapes were handled, but also the same shapes enclosed in a transparent plastic globe which was touched while they were visually presented. In both conditions these shapes were remembered better than shapes presented only visually. The experiments on depth perception with children aged 9 months (Walk and Gibson, 1959), and those on size, shape, brightness and pattern perception by Fantz (1965) have on the whole indicated that human infants see those dimensions in a similar way to adults, and show the same preference for complexity, symmetry and colour as older children. One should, however, remember that in regard to work on neonates White and Held (1966) found that prior to 1 month of age, infants failed to show visual accommodation responses to changes in target distance. Perfect visual accommodation was only attained by the fourth month. These results, together with observations indicating that convergence is very poorly developed below the age of $2\frac{1}{2}$ months, raise questions about the validity of the findings on form perception or visual activity in neonates.

Smith *et al.* (1963) concluded from the results of an experiment concerned with sensory feedback in young children, that feedback occurred first from postural, later from transport, and finally from manipulative movements. Smith and Wango (1963) also carried out a study in which they demonstrated that 11- and 12-year-olds were better able to adapt to inverted reversed visual feedback than were 9- to 11-year-olds. However, as Wohlwill (1966) points out, the conclusion (Smith and Greene, 1963) that this points to a critical period for the development of this function seems unjustified from these results.

In an ingenious series of observations concerning sensory integration, White et al. (1964) followed up Piaget's (1952) original observation on the development of the gaze-directed reaching response. Piaget saw this action as a manifestation of the adaptive growth of intelligence, that is of the capacity of the child to structure the results of his own actions. Development of intelligence takes place, according to him, as the child progressively modifies mental structures, which in turn alter the way in which he will both perceive and respond to the environment subsequently. White et al. (1964) investigated the process of visuo-motor development until the accurate reaching response was established more rigorously, but their conclusions are similar. After visual accommodation has appeared, the child discovers his own hands and spends much of his time in following their movements with his eyes. Swiping at objects with closed fists is followed by bringing the hand into the vicinity of the object, and subsequently by alternation of glance between them and their contact. This stage, which is seen during the fourth month, had also been observed by Piaget. In the fifth month, the child is able to integrate the visual information with his movements and reaches and grasps objects simply and accurately.

Held (1965) has stressed the necessity of response movements for the adequate utilization of visual information. Riesen and Aaron (1959) showed that visually guided behaviour in cats and chimpanzees was deficient when animals were reared from birth under conditions of restricting movements when in the light. Held and Hein (1963), in a classical experiment, compared kittens, some of which were allowed to move normally while the others were transported passively over an identical path, thus providing equal visual stimulation. Those who were moved passively failed at first to develop normal spatial capacities, though as Wohlwill (1966) points out, they soon caught up. In further experiments Held and Freedman (1963) showed that uncorrelated or conflicting information from the visual and motor systems led to a deterioration of performance. Held thinks that self-produced movements are necessary for adaptation and compensation in such conditions of visual distortions. Harris (1963, 1965) concludes that his results support the view that in conditions of distorted vision, changes in tactual perception occur, thus implying that the visual information is dominant. While his subjects gradually adjusted pointing movements to a visually displaced target, there was little or no transfer when he asked them to point with the other, hitherto unpractised hand. Harris holds that adaptation to optical distortion is a result of changes in the sense of position of the limbs, the head and the eyes. Rock and Victor (1963) share the view that there is strong evidence for a theory that vision is dominant in the interpretation of conflicting sensory information. Their experiments demonstrated that if conflicting visual and tactile information is presented to a subject, the interpretation will be made in accordance with the visual data. Thus subjects who had viewed a cube through a reducing prism, while feeling it at the same time with their hands, drew as well as matched it later to conform to the visual image. Likewise, subjects who viewed a square they held in their hands through a distorting prism, which gave it the visual appearance of a rectangle, said that the shape felt the same as it looked, i.e. a rectangle.

Howard and Templeton (1966) maintain that during adaptation the site of recalibration is a function of the response required and the information provided. They argue that there are two stages in adaptation to discordant information. One is the inhibition of the old, now inappropriate response, and the other the subsequent substitution of a new habit. Any information about displacement or distortion helps the subject to make this adaptation. Though such information is most often, and possibly also most effectively provided by active movement, knowledge of results alone leads at least to partial adaptation, even in conditions where such movement is absent. Recalibration seems to occur in that system for which training and information is provided.

For children, the effects of activity on adaptation to distorted vision were found to be similar to those in adults (Pick and Hay, 1966). No age trend between subjects of 8, 12 and 16 years in adapting responses to a visually displaced target was found by Held and Hein (1958). Thus, whatever the processes responsible for adaptation to prismatic distortions are, they seem not dependent on age.

Rock and Harris (1967) make inferences from their results about the hierarchical structure of the senses during early development. They think that there is no reason for believing that the separate tactile and position components of touch are innately organized into an impression of a solid object with a particular shape, but that there is considerable evidence to assume that vision is well developed at birth or soon after. Held and Hein (1963) and White and Held (1966) also think that the result from adaptation experiments are relevant for one's view of development. Held states: "When it can be shown that adaptation proceeds to a stable end state which corresponds to accurate orientation in the environment, then it is conceivable that the same process operates in the development of co-ordination in the new born infant." Held's (1961) view is that the organism acquires a built-in programme for correlating sensory data through active experience. According to this, a command for a motor movement is accompanied by a "copy" of the normally achieved visual result. The visual information which results from the movement is then fed back and compared with the visual data which was expected on the basis of the results of previous movements. In this way an expectation in regard to correlated visual and movement information is built up.

A shift in feedback from any one source will lead to the gradual working out of new correlations and then behaviour will adapt. Normally, we can expect a high degree of predictability that is constant over time, in the relation between particular efferent and reafferent signals in the nervous system. If the normal environment were to be replaced by one of continually shifting visual objects, whose movements were unrelated to any sensory–motor feedback, the result would be uninterpretable "noise". Hein and Held (1962) speculated that this condition of "noise" may be approximated by a blank visual field, which allows noise intrinsic to the visual nervous system to become the dominant signal. Both conditions would make it impossible for the system to organize incoming signals in correspondence with the external, environmental structure.

It is one advantage of an explanation of behaviour in terms of such models, that a behavioural impairment can in turn be explained by a breakdown of the hypothetical relevant mechanism.

Sensory Dominance in Autistic Children

As had been said, all autistic children had learned to discriminate between a box on a higher and one on a lower plane. One aspect of this learning task was that in addition to visual position cues, the relevant response movement towards the two boxes was also differential. In one instance an upward-reaching movement had to be made in order to obtain the reward, while a straight ahead arm movement was not rewarded. For alternate subjects the reverse was the case. These additional motor cues might have facilitated discrimination learning. The relevance of such additional motor activity for subnormals has been demonstrated by House (1964). As has already been mentioned, clinical observation suggests that autistic children rely considerably on information from proximal receptors. We have already discussed the notion of a hierarchical organization of sensory channels and suggested that information via certain sensory channels may be responded to more readily than data provided from other sources. The following experiments were aimed at establishing the relative responsiveness of autistic children to stimuli in different sensory modalities.

In the first of these studies (Hermelin and O'Connor, 1964), ten autistic and ten subnormal children were compared. They were matched for chronological age, which ranged from 8 to 16 years, with a mean age of 11 years 8 months. The children were also matched for perceptual motor ability on the Seguin formboard, which gave MAs between 3 and 12 years, mean 7 years 6 months. All children in this experiment obtained a minimum verbal comprehension MA of 2 years 9 months.

The subjects, who were tested individually, sat at a table with a vertical hardboard screen in front of them. In the upper left- and right-hand corners of this screen were lights which could be switched on, and on the back of the board, behind the lights, buzzers were placed. These were the visual and auditory stimuli. Pieces of string were tied lightly around each of the children's ankles, and the experimenter holding the ends of the string could give a slight tug on either side, which provided tactile stimulation as well as some induced movement. As the child's feet were obscured from his view by the table, no additional visual cues were provided. At each trial, two stimuli in different modalities and from different sides were presented simultaneously. A buzz on the right for instance, might occur together with a light from the left, or a tug on the left ankle together with a light from the right side. The child was told that whenever he saw, felt or heard a signal, he could obtain a sweet from a box on the same side from which the stimulus came, and demonstrations were given. As two stimuli, in fact, were always given simultaneously, and were thus in competition, it was left to the subject to select one or the other, and determine the direction of his response accordingly. There were no "incorrect" responses, and all were rewarded. In order to familiarize the children with the procedure, each subject was presented successively with each of the three stimuli on their own, either on his right or his left side. When stimulation occurred on the right, the subject could obtain a sweet by lifting the lid of a box on the right; when on the left, the reward also came from the left. In the experimental session following this, the subject could select whether to take the stimulus from the right or from the left as his cue for the placing of the reward. The data were investigated for position habits independent of signal modality, as well as for a tendency for selecting according to one sensory modality rather than another. The total number of responses to such bimodal stimulus presentation are shown in Table 4.

This table shows clearly that both groups responded predominantly to light whenever a visual stimulus was a component in the combination of

TABLE 4. NUMBER OF RESPONSES TO BIMODAL
STIMULUS PRESENTATION

Stimulus conditions	Number of responses (optimal 200)	
	Autistic	Controls
Sound	26	18
Light	174	182
Touch	48	2
Light	152	198
Sound	53	168
Touch	147	32

signals. If the combination was one of induced movement and visual signals, the autistic children, though still obtaining a clearly dominant light score, responded more frequently to the feedback of the induced movement than the controls, for whom such a response was very rare. A comparison of response patterns to simultaneous sound and movement stimulation resulted in a highly significant interaction. While the subnormal children gave more responses which were determined by sound than by passive movement, the reverse was true of the autistic children. Thus the relative dominance of the visual channel seems to have been equally established in the autistic as well as in the subnormal group. Auditory stimulation was more dominant than feedback from passive movement in the subnormal group, while the autistic children responded more often to such feedback than they did to sound. Similar preference for tactile responses in autistic children has subsequently been found by Schopler (1966).

In the next experiment (O'Connor and Hermelin, 1965b) the stimuli consisted of a light source in one corner of a room, which was presented simultaneously with either "white noise" or the words "come here" from the other corner. In this study, the aim was to control the intensities of the competing stimuli relative to each other. In the previous experiment this had not been done. Light and sound stimuli were equated on a scale of decibels suggested by Stevens and Galanter (1957). Fourteen autistic children and twenty-eight subnormals took part. The subnormal children were subdivided into fourteen mongol and fourteen non-mongoloid subjects. The mean age of the autistic group was 13 years 1 month, SD 2 years 10 months. The controls had a mean age of 12 years 11 months, SD 2 years 7 months. The groups were matched for performance on the Seguin formboard test, on which the autistic, mongol and non-mongol children had mean mental age scores of 60 months, 57 months and 69 months respectively. These MA scores were statistically identical. The children were also tested on the Peabody Picture Vocabulary test. On this the mean mental age was 31 months for the autistic and 34 months for the mongol children. The non-mongol subjects scored significantly higher, obtaining a mean score of 56 months. In the experimental session, the children were tested individually in a room which was empty, except for loudspeakers and lights placed in the left- and in the right-hand corners of the room. The room was dimly lit, and three display combinations were presented. They were either a light from one side and simultaneously a sound or the words "come here" from the other side at an equal and medium level of intensity. Alternatively, the light was bright and presented together with the noise or the words at a low intensity of sound. Or lastly, the auditory stimuli were presented loudly, together with a low-intensity light. The stimulus combination are shown in Table 5.

TABLE 5. LIGHT AND SOUND (OR WORD)
INTENSITY COMBINATIONS

Light (db)	Sound or word (db)
92	67
79	79
67	92

An analysis of variance on the frequency of responses to one or the other stimulus source resulted in a highly significant difference between intensities, and in a groups-by-treatments interaction. Only the mongol and subnormal children gave significantly more response to light than sound stimulation. For all subjects, an increase in the intensity of the noise or the words relative to the light increased the number of responses towards sounds and words, and decreased those towards light. But even regardless of intensity, the non-mongol subnormals responded more readily to words than to noise when both were presented together with light. This difference between noise and words was not significant in the mongol and autistic groups. This result seems to be related to the verbal mental ages of the groups, a conclusion supported by a highly significant correlation between individual verbal mental ages and the difference score between the frequency of responses to sound and verbal stimuli.

Table 6 shows, that, though a loud sound in combination with a soft light led to an increase in sound orientated responses in all groups, the scores of the autistic children remain more evenly distributed under all modality and intensity combinations than those of the subnormals. Autistic children were more determined by the positioning of the stimulus source either to the right or left than by different intensities or different stimulus modalities.

TABLE 6. DOMINANCE EXPERIMENT
(Percentages of Sound or Word Choice Scores for Groups and Signal Intensities)

| | Sound and light signals | | | | Word and light signals | | | |
	Light intense	Light and sound equal	Sound intense	Total	Light intense	Light and word equal	Word intense	Total
Autistic	42	39	59	47	53	55	58	55
Imbecile	17	20	30	22	46	54	63	54
Mongol	7	11	45	21	21	24	49	31

We already mentioned other experimental evidence (Hermelin and O'Connor, 1965) which supports the conclusion that discriminations made on the basis of, and with the additional information from, motor movements, are easier for autistic children to learn than those which only varied along visual dimensions. In the experiment in which the lifting of one of two boxes was rewarded, we presented three tasks. One in which the boxes were in different positions, i.e. high and low, one where an arrow was painted on one box, while the other was left blank, and finally, one where the discrimination had to be made between an upward pointing arrow on one box, and a downward pointing one on the other. In this experiment, all children solved a task in which an upwards or straight ahead reaching movement was required to obtain the reward. As some of them were unable to learn to discriminate according to visual cues only, this supports the conclusion that the presence of additional kinesthetic cues makes learning easier for autistic children. It should be noted that we were not concerned here with the learning of a left–right position discrimination, but that left- and right-hand positions were varied randomly between the upper and lower box.

These results, taken together with the predominance of position responses in the previous experiments, are relevant to findings such as Warren's (1959, 1960) which suggest that learning a position discrimination may not depend on the same pattern of abilities as that required by visual discrimination. There also exist interspecies differences in the facility with which discrimination problems in various sensory dimensions are solved. Warren reports that monkeys quickly learned to discriminate two different objects, provided these remained in the same position throughout, so that object cues and position cues coincided. Cats, on the other hand, learned to discriminate faster according to position when the two objects did not differ visually, thus learning better with one than with two relevant cues. In the next series of experiments, we tested whether position discrimination would be of varying difficulty according to whether an irrelevant dimension was or was not introduced. We also compared normal and autistic children on the relative ease of acquiring a position or a visual discrimination (Hermelin and O'Connor, 1967a).

The subjects were thirty-two autistic and thirty-two normal children. The mean CA of the autistic group was 11 years, ranging from 6 to 15 years. The normal children were matched with these subjects according to their scores on the Seguin formboard, and had a mean CA of 4 years 4 months, ranging from 3 years 3 months to 5 years 1 month.

The first task with which the children were individually presented was to select the one of four upturned aluminium boxes which concealed a sweet. The boxes were 1 inch high, with a width of 1.5 inches. They differed from each other in length by a constant amount of 1 inch, the shortest being 3 inches and the longest 6 inches in length. The four boxes were placed in front of the child in a line on a table, with a distance of 4 inches between any two. Sixteen children from each group had to solve a position discrimination problem, and sixteen were presented with a visual discrimination task. The groups were further subdivided into those for whom the extreme right- or left-hand positions, or the half right or half left positions were correct for the position-learning task. Likewise, in the visual discrimination task half the subjects had to learn to select the longest or shortest box and the other subjects had to select one or the other of the middle-sized boxes.

For the first trial the experimenter placed a sweet under the correct stimulus box in full view of the subject, who was then asked to find it. After this a screen was interposed between each of the forty-nine subsequent trials, while the boxes were rearranged. No correction for an incorrect response was allowed at any one time, and the child was simply told to try again next time.

When the data were analysed, it was found that the normal children learned all tasks significantly faster than the autistic ones. There was also a highly significant difference between tasks; the position discrimination was learned faster by all children than the length discrimination task. A significant interaction between serial position and task indicated that this difference between tasks was more marked when the correct stimuli for length discrimination were of middle size. If the correct response consisted of selecting the shortest or longest of the boxes, the difference between visual and position problems was less marked.

Having established that autistic and young normal children learned responses to position cues more readily than to visual ones, we asked whether the presence or absence of other irrelevant distinguishing features of the stimuli would affect position learning. As already mentioned, different species of animals give different answers to this question. Some seem to be helped and some hindered by visual variation in the learning of position habits. In the first experiment, we had used a procedure which compared the relative ease of learning to discriminate along the dimension of length or of position. In each of these tasks one of these two variables was the relevant and the other the irrelevant stimulus aspect. In the second experiment, we compared the learning of two tasks: in the first, four boxes of different length were again presented, and a reward was always placed under a box in a certain position. As the stimuli were rearranged from trial to trial, the length of this box varied between trials. If, for instance, the reward was to be found under the second box from the right, on one trial this might be the smallest, on the next trial the second largest might be in that position, and so on. However, the respective length of a particular box was irrelevant for the solving of the problem. The second task used four boxes of identical length, so that position was the only discriminable, as well as the relevant, factor. In this experiment the autistic children needed more trials to learn to criterion than did the normals, but there was no difference between the tasks. For both groups the number of trials needed to learn up to the criterion of nine correct responses out of ten was statistically the same, whether the boxes differed in length or not.

Though visual cues do play a part, position discrimination is essentially the learning of a motor habit, and may be thought of as the organization of movement or output. Because of the apparent imperception of many psychotic children on the one hand, and their relatively intact motor capacity on the other, we had predicted that normals would be better than psychotics in learning a length discrimination, while the reverse might be the case in position discrimination learning. This prediction would result in a groups-by-conditions interaction in an analysis of variance, which, in fact, was not present in the results. Normals as well as psychotics found it easier to learn the positions than to learn the length discrimination, and the difference in scores between those conditions was the same for both groups. Therefore an interpretation of the results must be thought of in developmental rather than in clinical terms. The organization of motor movements and the analysis of kinesthetic feedback may provide additional information for young, immature children. This information will reinforce data coming from visual cues, and thus facilitate discrimination learning. This does not imply that position responses arise from motor cues alone and are independent of visual cues. The dependence of position habits on such visual cues was demonstrated by White and Plumm (1962) who found that they were preceded by glances towards the position responded to. Relevant results from subnormal (House 1964) and animal (Warren, 1959, 1960) learning support such an interpretation.

Turning to the length discrimination problem, those subjects who did solve the tasks did so in fewer trials if the correct stimulus was either the longest or shortest of the series. An explanation for this may be given in terms of Inhelder and Piaget (1958), describing an experiment where children are presented with a collection of sticks of different length. The longest of these is placed in front of the child and he is asked to draw the one that comes next in length, then the next and so on to the shortest of the series. Children who were able to do this were yet unable to produce such a series by using the sticks rather than drawing them. Inhelder and Piaget explain these results by pointing out that the actual seriation involves reversibility, while making the drawing does not. In making the drawing, the child only has to make a single comparison: i.e. each line has to be shorter than the one preceding it. On the other hand, in actually ordering the elements, each one except the tallest and the shortest is shorter than some and longer than other sticks. Thus a simultaneous comparison has to be made, where a certain stick is both shorter than the ones already in the series and longer than those that remain to be ordered. The required operation thus becomes multidirectional or reversible. This interpretation applies directly to our findings. The shortest and longest of the boxes are shorter or longer than all the three remaining ones and a unidirectional comparison is all that is needed. Each of the two boxes of intermediate length on the other hand is longer than some and shorter than others, and a multidirectional comparison is needed to solve the problem. The difference between the performance on the two types of length discrimination tasks—i.e. intermediate and extreme lengths—is therefore explicable in terms of cognitive stages of development.

Sensory Integration

The last results indicated that young normal and autistic children attended to one of two varying stimulus dimensions only, ignoring the other.

The next two experiments carried out in collaboration with Frith, tested the extent to which autistic and normal children differ in performing motor tasks carried out with or without visual guidance. We asked to what extent autistic children would use information from distance receptors (vision) and whether they would be able to integrate visual with kinaesthetic information. Such integration may depend on the maturational developmental stage reached by children, as has been suggested by Birch and Lefford (1963). All subjects were therefore given a visual–motor test (Frostig, 1961) for perceptual development, which allows the calculation of a "perceptual age" (PA). On the basis of these test results, the children, whose CAs ranged from 4 to 16 years, were divided into groups with higher, and groups with lower PA. The relevant data are given in Table 7. As one would expect, the CAs and PAs for normals correspond closely, and a weak but significant relationship exists for the autistic children.

TABLE 7. CHRONOLOGICAL AND PERCEPTUAL AGES OF SUBJECTS IN
TRACKING AND PUZZLE EXPERIMENTS

		Normal	Autistic
Low level	$\overline{X}$ CA	4.3	9.4
	Range	3.9–4.0	6.3–14.1
	$\overline{X}$ PA	4.1	3.11
	Range	3.6–4.9	2.9–4.6
High level	$\overline{X}$ CA	6.0	10.10
	Range	5.4–6.0	7.11–15.2
	$\overline{X}$ PA	6.3	6.5
	Range	5.0–9.4	5.0–10.0

For the first experiment, the task consisted in guiding a metal stylus inside a 2 millimetre wide groove cut out of 6 millimetre thick perspex. There were 5 tracks of equal length (24 inches). One of these (a) was used for practice only. The others were of an increasing degree of complexity, and are shown in Fig. 3. Each track had a microswitch fitted at the end. The experimenter started an electric clock at the beginning of each trial, and contact between the stylus and the switch at the end of the track switched off the clock. A time score for each "run" was thus obtained. The tasks were carried out under two conditions, one in which the child had a full view of the track and of his own hand and arm movements, and one in which such a view was prevented by tying an apron around the neck of the child and attaching the other end to a metal frame at a distance of 11 inches and at about 10 inches above the display. This enabled the child to move his hands and arms freely underneath this cover, and at the same time prevented him from seeing the track and his arms and hands.

Verbal instructions were minimal, and the emphasis was put on demonstration and practice. Practice on the practice track was given with and without vision. The preferred hand was always used. Each child completed the task in both conditions, alternate children doing it either with or without vision first.

The first analysis of variance of the time scores showed that for both conditions and for all tracks children with a high PA were significantly faster than those with a lower PA. The analysis also demonstrated that all children were faster when looking at the tracks than when not looking. However, this difference between conditions with and without vision was significantly greater for the normal than autistic children, statistical analysis resulting in a highly significant interaction. All groups were statistically identical in their performance when looking at the tracks, but the normals were significantly slower than the autistic when not looking. This is illustrated in Fig. 4. For all groups the advantage of looking was greater for the more complex tracks than it was for the simple ones. When the groups are subdivided according to PA rather than according to diagnosis, similar differences result. Children with higher PA show a greater difference between conditions with and without vision than do children with lower PAs. Children with lower and higher PAs are not different from each other on tracking without visual guidance, but with visual guidance the more advanced children profit relatively more. Those children who had first tracked with visual guidance were no better than those who carried out the task first without vision. This was true for both groups, and is consistent with results reported by Zaporozhets (1961). He found that showing children a finger maze before they had to trace it blindfold, did not improve performance with children up to age 6. Older children did better when they were first shown the maze.

It should be noted that improvement with visual guidance was in terms of speed, as there was no possibility of making errors. This improvement in speed with visual guidance may be due to some planning process, e.g. looking ahead. Vision enables the subjects to anticipate the next corner and thus to make certain muscular adjustments in advance. It seems that autistic children rely less on this planning function than normals.

The next experiment followed up these conclusions. In this investiga-

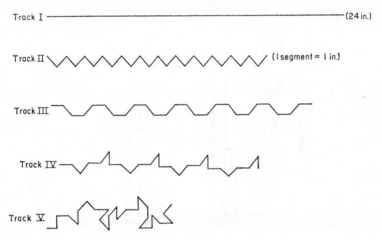

FIG. 3. Tracks for Tracking experiment.

tion, three tasks were used, which are illustrated in Fig. 5. In the first, six straight-edged cards, 3.3 by 5.0 centimetres had to be arranged so that a continuous line resulted, which was drawn in segments on the individual card. The second condition used cards, of which the sides were cut out in jigsaw puzzle-type edges. As no guiding line was drawn on them, and the edges were difficult to distinguish visually, the main cue for assembling was whether or not they fitted into one another. This was best established by trial and error manipulation. The third task used cards with similar jagged edges, but with segments of a line drawn on each card, which would run continuously if the segments were fitted together correctly. The three tasks thus provided varying degrees of a combination of visual and motor cues. The same children as in the previous experiment acted as subjects.

The child was given the six segments for any one task and was required to put them into a frame so as to construct a continuous line running

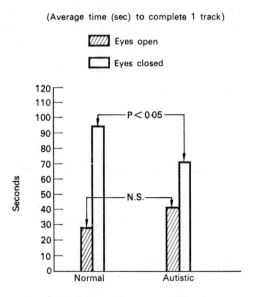

FIG. 4. Tracking with open and closed eyes.

through and/or to fit the interlocking edges of the cards together. Demonstrations were given by the experimenter, and the first of a series was placed in the frame by the experimenter at the beginning of each trial. Three trials were given on each task, and order of presentation of tasks was randomly varied across subjects according to a balanced design. Time needed to complete a series was recorded. If a wrong card were selected, the experimenter put it back and said, "No, that's wrong, try another one".

Analysis of variance of the results showed that as in the previous experiment, children with higher PAs were significantly faster in all conditions than children with lower PAs. The analysis also showed that

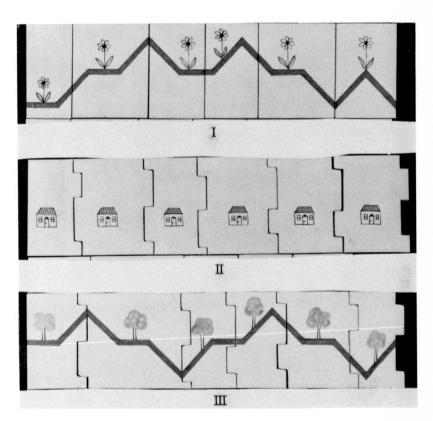

Fig. 5. Material for puzzle experiment.

the autistic children were significantly faster than the normal ones and also made fewer errors. Overall performance on the straight-edged cards with the continuous line was fastest, and performance on the jigsaw-type cards without design, slowest. The analysis also resulted in a highly significant interaction between PA and diagnostic groups. This interaction indicates that all normal as well as more advanced autistic children carried out a task with the help of a predominantly visual strategy more efficiently than one in which such visual cues are minimal. However, this is not true for the more backward autistic children. They perform equally well with those cards on which visual cues are minimal and those containing both the visual information as well as motor cues. They are worst on the task depending most clearly on a visually determined strategy. The results are illustrated in Fig. 6.

It seems that with increasing development, performance and strategy of autistic children become more like that of normals of comparative developmental level. With the more retarded autistic children, qualitative differences in approaching visual–motor tasks are apparent and are mainly characterized by an inability to integrate cues from different modalities, and by more efficient use of data arising from trial and error movements, than from visual information. In the first of these last two experiments, autistic children benefited significantly less from additional visual information than did normals. In the second of these studies autistic children of low perceptual-motor age were favoured by conditions in which visual information was minimal and manipulative cues maximal. These experiments lend support to the hypothesis that autistic children who function on a low developmental level are more impaired in extracting visual than motor information, and that all autistic children are less able than normals at a similar stage of perceptual motor development, to utilize vision as a planning function for perceptual motor tasks.

SUMMARY

Abnormal response behaviour to sensory stimulation has been observed in many autistic children. Such abnormalities are most frequently found in responses to auditory stimulation, but also occur with visual stimuli. Preference for exploration through the proximal receptor channels has been reported, and attention has been drawn to similar behaviour in children who are not autistic but suffer from various specific handicaps. In accounting for perceptual abnormalities, factors such as orientation deficits, inability to name the stimuli and a differential responsiveness of different sensory systems may be relevant. Though some investigators of normal children have formed a view of a gradual developmental change from proximal to distance receptor dominance, recent experiments with

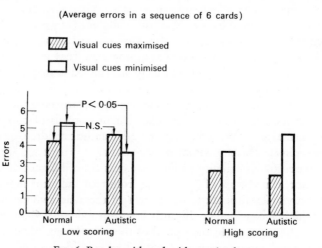

(Average errors in a sequence of 6 cards)

FIG. 6. Puzzles with and without visual cues.

normal infants indicate selective responsiveness to visual and auditory stimuli soon after birth. While some authors have supported a theory of leading or dominant senses, others have put more emphasis on integration and correlation of incoming sense data from various sources.

Our experiments showed that selective fixation of simultaneously presented visual displays was similar in autistic and young normal children. All looked longer at a coloured than at a black, a striped than a grey and a meaningful than a random display. However, the autistic children fixated all stimuli for a significantly shorter period than the controls and made fewer comparisons than the normals.

In another experiment, in which an operant discrimination response was required, we found that speaking autistic children needed more trials

to learn shape and directional discriminations than those involving brightness or size. No such differences were found with the normals. Non-
speaking autistic children could solve none of these discrimination tasks.
Non-speaking autistic children could also not discriminate between an
upward- and a downward-pointing arrow. Some non-speaking children
also failed to learn to distinguish a box which had an arrow painted on it,
from one which was blank. We also found that autistic children needed
more trials to solve a length discrimination problem than did normals.

In testing the hierarchical structure of sensory dominance in experiments using bimodal simultaneous stimulation, we found that autistic,
subnormal and normal children responded most often to a light, rather
than to a sound or a slight induced movement. While subnormal and
normal children responded more often to sound than to passive movement, the reverse was true of the autistic subjects. In another study where
intensity as well as stimulus dimension were varied, softly spoken words
evoked more responses than a simultaneously presented bright light with
non-mongol subnormals, while the reverse was the case in pairing the light
with noise. Mongol and autistic children who had lower verbal IQs
reacted similarly to words and sounds. Their responses were less determined by the mode of stimulation than by position and the intensity of
the stimuli.

When visual discrimination tasks were arranged in such a way that
distinct movement response cues were available, autistic children performed as well as normals at a similar level of mental development. This
was demonstrated in experiments in which an upward or forward reaching movement and in another in which a left–right position response was
required.

Our results indicate that while the perception of differences seems
relatively unimpaired in autistic children, attention towards visual stimuli
is not sustained, few comparisons between such stimuli are made, and
perhaps consequently the processing and utilisation of visually presented
data is deficient. On the other hand, it seems from our results that feedback
information from response movements is more readily analysed. Put
more simply, doing something different to different things provides more
information than perceptual input alone. This is probably so for every-
body, but the normal or relatively mature organism can readily adopt
other strategies to analyse input when this should become appropriate.

But purely visual and possibly also auditory input, in the absence of co-ordinated response activity is not sufficient for discrimination performance in autistic children.

The minimal utilization of visual information by autistic children was further demonstrated by the results of a tracking experiment with and without visual guidance. The difference between these two conditions was far greater for the normal than for the autistic children, particularly with the more complex tasks. Normal children performed a tracking task much better when they could see what they were doing than when they could not. Autistics were as fast as the normals without vision, but much slower when the track was visible. Another study presented tasks of which one could be solved only by using visual cues. For another, visual information was not easily usable and this task could best be solved by trial-and-error manipulation. Autistic children with a higher level of perceptual development and all normal children were best on the task at which visual cues were maximal. On the other hand, the autistic children with lower PAs were fastest, and made the least number of errors in conditions which favoured trial-and-error manipulation. All these results lend support to a hypothesis, which links the clinically observed preference of autistic children for proximal receptors to a tendency to process and make use of information from induced and active movements. In other words the children seem to rely more on perceptual activity than on perceptual analysis. Though there are similar tendencies with young normal children, as for instance in the facility to learn position discriminations, the autistics seem less able to use alternative strategies when these would be more appropriate. This is particularly apparent in those autistic children who function on a lower level of linguistic and perceptual development. If problems are such that this relative independence from visual information can be used to advantage, the performance of the autistic child may actually be better than that of normal children at a similar stage of mental develop-ment. But more often efficient performance depends on the integration and intercorrelation of input and output data, and on the processing of information from various sources. It is this function which seems impaired in autistic children, and leads to their apparently abnormal response behaviour to sensory stimuli.

CHAPTER 3

LANGUAGE, CODING, SERIATION AND RECALL

LANGUAGE DEVELOPMENT IN CHILDREN

It is beyond the scope of this book to attempt a review of the research on the development of language in children. There have been many well controlled experiments, but much work is also based on observations in natural settings. The question of how language is acquired by the child is still a controversial one. However, the sequence of acquisition and its relation to stages of development is well established. By the end of the third month of life, the child has begun to "babble", i.e. to produce random vocalization, at first mainly vowel-like pitch-modulated, sounds. This increases throughout the first year in amount and diversity. At about 5 months some consonants appear. Sound types are generally produced in random order and have little relation to later language development. In fact, when babbling stops the child seems to have lost the ability to produce certain sounds, at least temporarily, and in speech development proper phonemes re-emerge in a certain pre-determined order. There thus seems to be a discontinuity between babbling and the beginning of speech, a fact reinforced by the observation that congenitally deaf children babble normally for a limited period.

Between the ages of 8 and 10 months, the child begins to imitate sound patterns and even before that shows signs of understanding words and sentences. Lewis (1936) suggests that intonation patterns in sentences are probably the earliest items to be distinguished. It may be relevant that many of the higher animals can also learn to distinguish a limited number of intonation patterns in human speech.

At about the end of the first year, active voluntary use of language has begun, though understanding is for many years, and perhaps always, far in

61

advance of production. Between 12 and 18 months, utterances are often learned as whole units consisting of several words. This is also the period of one-word sentences. A single word can appear in a variety of situational contexts, which would have elicited a number of different utterances from an adult. Similarly, one word can appear in linguistic contexts, which for an adult would imply different grammatical parts of speech.

Between the second and third years there is a rapid and vast increase in vocabulary. Two-word sentences at 2 years have given place to nearly colloquial grammar at 5. By the age of about 6, the child's ability to manipulate syntactical structures seems nearly complete, though vocabulary growth does continue. Development of articulation ability, sentence length and grammar are strongly related. There is some evidence (Templin, 1957), that mean sentence length is equal or similar to immediate memory span between the ages of 3 and 7.

The main lines of thinking about how language is acquired are those based on theories of conditioning, notably Skinner's (1957), and those stressing a more biologically oriented approach, such as Lenneberg's (1967). Skinner's position is well known, and has the great advantage that it brings language acquisition into line with other types of learning without requiring additional constructs. However, a conditioning type theory seems to be insufficient to account for the acquisition of grammatical rules. Another line of reasoning and research sees language acquisition as only one aspect of general cognitive development. According to this view, channels other than the auditory-vocal could be used for decoding and encoding processes, in cases where language impairment has occurred, but intact cognitive functioning has been maintained.

The complexity of even such relatively simple processes as naming and labelling, is illustrated in models such as those of Feigenbaum (1963), Hunt (1962) or Oldfield (1966). In such models the assigning of a meaning for a word is thought to proceed on lines analogous to a binary, hierarchical computer operation. It depends on the identification and reidentification of stimuli, comparing them with previously stored data on a match–mismatch basis. Whenever input received and tested does not match the stored encoded pattern, a further encoding is required, to represent a further choice point of comparison. Arriving at a positive decision, i.e. "match", assumes assigning an input to a sub-set of objects or events. Such an operation depends on at least two processes. (1) Perception of the varied stimulus dimensions on encountering a stimulus on a number of occasions and in different forms and settings; (2) the selection of a subset of dimensions, representing the recurrent relevant common patterns in the incoming messages. For example, to decide whether an x is an X, a match–mismatch comparison would have to be made before x could be named "X". For this operation, the goodness of fit of the properties of the stimulus input and the specification of the category "X" would have to be tested. A breakdown in this process could occur at various points. There might be an inadequacy in scanning the input, so that on each encounter a new coding process would occur, which would fail to overlap with that made on a previous occasion. In other words, there would be a failure of recognition. Alternatively, the deficit might arise from too many stimuli being coded as a defining set for a label. This would lead to too many objects or events being represented by a given word. Finally, there could be an inability to make correct "match–mismatch" decisions, so that an object would be assigned a category having an inappropriate label. That would lead to misnaming.

An associative model of the learning of grammar is suggested by Braine (1963). This assumes that grammatical structures are acquired through a process of contextual generalization. The child is held to learn the position of word units within a sequence, as well as making associations between pairs of morphemes. These learned units are primarily phrases, and sequences of primary phrases. Their locations within sentences are learned through becoming familiar with sound units in the temporal positions in which they occur. Braine himself states that such a system could only account for the acquisition of a very simple "kernel" grammar. Certainly the learning of sequential probabilities alone would not enable one either to understand or to produce meaningful speech. This has been demonstrated by Miller (1964), and is stressed in a linguistic analysis such as Chomsky's (1961, 1965). Lenneberg (1967) argues against a piecemeal learning of linguistic items, but his stressing of the biological basis of language development is descriptive rather than explanatory.

The factors pointing to maturation rather than learning at the beginning of language development are, according to him, the regularity in the sequence of language acquisition, and its uniform beginning between the eighteenth and the twenty-eighth month of life, the synchronization with other functions clearly attributable to physical maturation, and the indication for a critical period of primary language acquisition. Though the role of environmental factors and practice is acknowledged, they are not regarded as crucial. Thus children of deaf parents were observed to babble normally when they became able to do so. At a later stage of development the maturational factor is stressed by the results of a study by Dennis and Najarian (1957) who found orphanage children below average in language ability at the age of 3, but normal by the time they were 6.

The worsening of prognosis with advancing age in acquired aphasia, the universality of the developmental sequences of language acquisition, and the rapidity with which such a complex function is perfected, support Lenneberg's point of view. So does the fact that children seem to use linguistic rules and categories at an early stage of language development. The many studies of children's grammar bear this out. Berko (1958), for instance, presented 4- to 7-year-olds with nonsense words and asked them to transform these into plurals, their past and future tenses, possessives and compound verbs. Though the answers did not always conform to English usage, they nevertheless demonstrated that children in this age range operated with clearly defined morphological rules. Answers between different age groups were not qualitatively different. Even the youngest children did not treat new words idiosyncratically. The picture was one of consistency, regularity and simplicity.

The grammatical rules which children use in their speech are thus not simply based on an imitation of adult speech. On the contrary, they include many instances never used in adult language. Examples of this are the changes in those rules, occurring with age, which govern negations or past tenses. Such rules are spontaneously generated and are gradually adjusted, rather than simply imitated.

Research taking account of such observations has received impetus from the theories of Chomsky (1957, 1965). Particularly in the earlier version of this theory, grammar appeared to be regarded as a self-contained system which was relatively independent of semantics. The more recent account attempts to interrelate semantics, grammar and phonology. In so far as Chomsky's views are relevant for the study of first language acquisition, his contributions include his advocacy of major innate components in language development, the expansion of the concept of the generating of grammatical rules, and his insistence on its centrality in the language process. Grammar, as Chomsky points out, is not explicable in terms of learned sequential contingencies, and the understanding and production of sentences cannot therefore be explained through probability learning. Different sentences, with an equal probability of contiguity between the words they contain, can nevertheless be appreciated as being either more or less grammatically correct. Contiguity of parts of speech instead of single words is an equally inadequate set of axioms for language structure. Instead, what is necessary for understanding and producing language is a set of rules concerning the relationships of different grammatical patterns, i.e. active, passive, declarative, interrogative, negative, etc. These relationships are the rules of transformation, and they are applied to the analysis of input data as well as for the planning and organizing of the output. Thus knowing the language depends on the acquisition of a set of organizing principles.

Such a point of view is, of course, highly relevant for one's interpretation of language deficits. If one accepts a conditioning-type theory as appropriate, one will use remedial teaching and behaviour therapy, such as that employed with some success by Lovaas (1966) with autistic children. If, on the other hand, language behaviour is regarded as depending specifically on biological prerequisites, one might favour research specifying relevant physiological impairments. In either case, "language deficit" is too general a term to be useful and the precise nature of such deficits needs to be specified by experiments.

LANGUAGE DEFICITS IN AUTISTIC CHILDREN

Perhaps the most striking, and certainly the most common impairment found in autistic children is their language deficit. Indeed, some investigators have suggested that this linguistic impairment may be the basic cause of their inability to structure the environment, as well as the reason for their inability to form meaningful human relationships. However, in our view, it would be mistaken to assume a single basic primary handicap such as the linguistic one. The autistic child, in contrast to deaf or aphasic children, suffers from multiple handicaps affecting many, and in severe cases, most channels of input and output. Children suffering from developmental aphasia also tend to show other behavioural abnormalities. Worster-Drought (1957) described one type of aphasia in children, which he calls "congenital auditory imperception". However, such children, though they may be unable to lip-read, will nevertheless learn to converse in sign language and gestures, using alternative symbols and signs for communication. Similarly, Furth (1966) has shown that deaf, speechless children can handle logical concepts, provided that implicit linguistic processes are irrelevant to the problem to be solved.

Luria (1961), holds that the failure of the mentally subnormal to connect the verbal with the motor system is responsible for much of their cognitive deficit. He and his colleagues take the view that the development of language turns simple differentiating–discriminating operations into reasoning processes, such as comparison and coding. It is held that the verbal system in the severely subnormal child does not develop sufficiently to assume this function. Luria states that words for such children remain only impelling, excitatory signals, inhibitory functions having failed to develop. A dissociation between verbal and motor systems results from these and other deficiencies. Stimulus–response connections which consequently tend to become established without verbal associations, are held to remain unstable and specific. In addition they may depend on constant reinforcements, and may disintegrate at a slight change in the manner of presenting the signals. Luria states that "as the system of verbal abstractions does not take its necessary role in the formation of new links in the severely subnormal, the child's psychological development must inevitably and increasingly take on a deeply pathological character on account of this defect".

Following Luria, many experiments, including our own (O'Connor and Hermelin, 1963a) have demonstrated the role of language in the cognitive development of severely subnormal children. Bryant (1965, 1967a, 1967b) assessed the effect of verbal instruction in visuo–motor learning and transfer tasks. Results of his experiments showed that learning was improved by general verbal instructions in both experimental and control groups. In the transfer tasks, however, verbal instruction during initial learning was no aid for the subnormals, although it did improve the performance of normal controls of matched mental age. Bryant concluded that imbeciles were not aided in discrimination tasks by general instructions concerning the relevance of one dimension over another, because their strategy was to eliminate false cues one by one, rather than attempting to select one correct one.

The interdependence of IQ and language development in childhood autism has been demonstrated by Rutter (1966a, 1966b). In his follow-up study of autistic children, he found a highly significant correlation between IQ and subsequent development of speech. Of 20 non-speaking autistic children with IQs of or below 55, only one acquired some speech at age 12. However, out of nine non-speaking children with IQs above 55, five subsequently developed speech. It seems from this study that the bad prognosis for autistic children without speech at 5 years of age, which has been reported by Eisenberg (1956), is mainly due to, or at least associated with, low general intelligence.

In most samples, between 30 and 50 per cent of autistic children are reported to have remained mute. Kanner (1950) found eight out of twenty-three autistic children remained without speech. Eisenberg (1956) reported thirty-one autistic children without speech at age 5 out of a total of sixty-three. In Rutter's (1966) sample of sixty-one autistic children, only ten gained a normal level of speech development, and twenty-nine remained mute. In Lotter's (1967) survey, nine out of thirty-two 8-year-olds were mute, and Mittler, Gillies and Jukes (1966) report that nine out of twenty psychotic children remained without useful speech. Even in those autistic children who do learn to talk, language development can never be said to be completely normal. The abnormalities and peculiarities of speech development take various forms, of which a limited vocabulary and echolalia are by far the most common. Short-term echolalia, i.e. the immediate repetition of the last words said by another speaker, are also common in subnormal children, but delayed echolalia is rather more typical of autism. A sentence such as "do you want a drink" is stored verbatim and reproduced by the child at a later date on which he means to ask for a drink. The repetition of such phrases often imitates the accent and intonation of the initial speaker.

As Kanner has pointed out, the pronominal reversal by the children, using "you" rather than "I" when talking about themselves, should also be regarded as an instance of echolalic speech, rather than as some indefinable "unawareness of their own identities". As the child is usually addressed as "you" or by his name, he will use these same forms when talking about himself. Many autistic children also have difficulties in learning to label things correctly. A child can be said to have understood the meaning of a word when it is uttered in relation to its appropriate stimulus. Autistic children, though understanding and using word pairs such as "brush and comb", "shoes and socks" or "mummy and daddy" nevertheless often have great difficulty in learning to associate the correct label of such a word-pair with the appropriate object. The children also make grammatical errors, such as saying "Let's take park to doggy". They may fail to understand complex phrasing, or may use their own metaphors for objects and events. Even with good speech development, language retains a characteristic literalness and concreteness. Kanner reported (1946) that the children were unable to accept synonyms of words, or different connotations of the same propositions. Phonological abnormalities of speech have also been noted. Autistic children have been reported to use peculiar "voices" on occasion, and Goldfarb (1961) noted an absence or inappropriateness of phonological stress, volume, pitch and intonation, which resulted in mispronunciation, sing-song, flatness or talking in whispers only.

In some autistic children, auditory imperception seems paralleled by a similar imperception of information from other sensory channels. This may take various forms. Firstly, the child may be unable to process auditory and visual or kinaesthetic and auditory information adequately, but may deal relatively competently with messages in less affected sensory modalities. In some children, responses to touch, taste, smell and vibration seem to be relatively little affected. Alternatively, certain basic mental processes, such as ordering, serialization, coding or abstraction may be impaired in regard to all channels, while other simpler operations may be quite competently dealt with in all modalities. The child may be able to appreciate music but not words, simple but not more complex sequences of movement, detail but not patterns, or numbers and quantities but not temporal sequences.

In the following experiments we are concerned with several aspects of language impairment in autism. In the first section, we will describe experiments, which are concerned with language-relevant processes, which are tested in the auditory–vocal channel as well as in other modalities. Thus we are asking the question whether the language impairment in autistic children is modality specific, as, for instance, in the deaf or aphasic, or whether underlying cognitive processes are generally affected.

Further on we will be particularly concerned with the appreciation of order and structure and its relation to grammar. We will also report experiments concerned with the semantic as well as with the phonological components of language.

LINGUISTIC CODING

Language behaviour is not a unitary process, but necessitates a multitude of operations, including those of coding, categorizing and association. An attempt to test some of these is made in the Illinois Test of Psycholinguistic Abilities. This test, by McCarthy and Kirk (1961), is based on a psycholinguistic model suggested by Osgood (1957a, 1957b) and comprises three main dimensions. These are (1) levels of organization, (2) psycholinguistic processes, and (3) channels of communication.

There are two levels of organization, the representational and the automatic sequential. On the representational level, the test is concerned with mediating activities, with the understanding of meaning and with linguistic symbols. On the automatic sequential level retention of sequences and automatic habit chains are tested. The processes involved are decoding, encoding and association. They can occur in any one sensory channel, i.e. verbal, visual and motor, or across channels.

On the representational level, tests of decoding are concerned with the understanding of words or pictures. Association processes are tested by relating one word or picture to another, and encoding is defined as the expression of ideas in words and gestures. Coding and association are tested in all channels. On the "automatic sequential level" meaning is not involved. This part of the test is concerned with only those aspects of language which become automatic through constant repetition. One verbal and one visual memory test are presented in this section, as well as one concerned with the familiarity of grammatical usage. As Osgood (1963) points out, a test based on such variables may enable one to distinguish decoding as distinct from encoding or association deficits. It may also reflect impairment at the level of either semantic or structural organization, and finally, may test the same processes across different sensory modalities.

In collaboration with us, Tubbs (1966) gave this test to ten subnormals, ten normals and ten autistic children. The groups were matched on their scores on the Peabody Picture Vocabulary, and their mental and chronological ages are given in Table 8. It can be seen from the table that the range of verbal development among the autistic group is larger than that found in the subnormals, in spite of a similar CA range.

TABLE 8. RANGE OF SUBJECTS' CHRONOLOGICAL AGES AND MENTAL AGES ACCORDING TO PEABODY VOCABULARY TEST

	CA range	Mean CA	MA range	Mean MA
Normal	3–2 to 4–9	4–1	1–8 to 5–11	4–5
Severely subnormal	9–0 to 16–11	13–3	2–2 to 5–11	4–5
Autistic	6–8 to 14–9	10–9	2–8 to 10–5	4–5

An analysis of variance of the scores obtained on the ITPA resulted in a highly significant groups difference, as well as in a highly significant groups-by-conditions interaction. Further testing of this interaction revealed that autistic children did not differ significantly from subnormals or younger normals in tests of visual decoding, visual–motor association and visual as well as verbal immediate memory. They were significantly worse in auditory–verbal decoding and association functions, and on verbal as well as on non-verbal encoding tests. They also differed from normal and subnormal children in their ability to handle grammar adequately.

Summing up the results on the ITPA for testing linguistic function on the semantic, representational level, one can state the following:

(1) Decoding processes: these are defined as "the sum total of those habits required to ultimately obtain meaning from either visual or auditory linguistic stimuli". Autistic children are significantly impaired in this when the decoding has to occur at the auditory–vocal level. However, they do not differ significantly from the controls when the material presented and the responses required are non-verbal.

(2) Association processes: defined as "the sum total of those habits required to manipulate linguistic symbols internally". As in the decoding tests, the autistic children differ from the normals in this function only when the tests are directly concerned with the use and association of words. When the same function is tested through the use of pictures or objects they perform similarly to the controls.

(3) Encoding processes: this is "the sum total of those habits required to ultimately express oneself in words or gestures". This function is severely impaired in autistic children in the verbal as well as the non-verbal channel, and they differ in this significantly from the subnormals as well as from the normals. While decoding and association processes are less deficient when words are not directly involved, the impairment in encoding seems to be a basic defect rather than a specific channel deficiency.

While the semantic, representational level of organization is concerned with meaning, the automatic sequential level tests grammar and retention. The "auditory–vocal automatic" subtest is concerned with the appreciation of grammar, and uses items like: "Here is one hat. Here are two . . ." Or: "Mother is writing a letter. This is the letter she has. . . ." On this test the autistic children though not significantly worse than the subnormals, differed significantly from the normal children. Further experiments will illustrate the autistic children have difficulties in making use of grammatical structure.

The results of the two memory tests are interesting, because they reverse the relative channel efficiency found in the semantic tests. The autistic children do better on the test in verbal than in visual form. In this they resemble the normals, who also have better verbal than visual memories, but not the subnormals, in whom these trends are reversed. While there is no significant difference in verbal immediate memory between any of the groups, the subnormals are significantly better than the autistic children on the visual memory test.

The results obtained from the normal and autistic children on the memory tests confirm findings with normal adults, that auditory storage is the most efficient. However, visual memory seems by no means a unitary function and further experiments will illustrate this.

Linguistic functions obviously include the use of symbols and concepts, the processes of categorizing and coding and the ability to communicate with others through the use and comprehension of such signs and symbols. Any system comprising these elements can be called a language, such as the morse code, the sign language used by the deaf, computer language, or the system of symbols for expressing propositions in symbolic logic. In a series of experiments, Furth (1964, 1966) has demonstrated that deaf children, though they have no speech, nevertheless use adequate logical and conceptual structures and processes in their thinking. Such logical structures as Piaget (1965) has demonstrated, develop relatively independently of language. Though Luria (1961) and Kendler and Kendler (1967) have attempted to demonstrate the dependence of logical operations on language and mediation, it seems that children are able to solve many problems at an operational stage before they can manipulate the relevant concepts verbally. Conversely, the ability to verbalize is not always accompanied by an ability to make problem solving behaviour correspond to verbal utterances, as shown by O'Connor and Hermelin (1959) and Bryant (1967). From our results on the ITPA, it seems that autistic children can manipulate non-verbal linguistic units in decoding and association processes at a level reached by 4- to 5-year-old normals. In encoding, i.e. in the expression and communication of ideas, the impairment affects verbal as well as non-verbal channels. This aspect of their language deficit could thus justifiably be called a communication impairment or an expressive impairment. However, there is no indication that this is in any way caused by an emotional or social aloofness or "aloneness" to use Kanner's term. If any causal relationship can be inferred, it points to a cognitive deficit, leading to an inability to acquire the skills which are essential for adequate social contact and communication. In an attempt to explore the nature of this presumed cognitive deficit, we tried to analyse its effect on visual material, assuming that the rules governing the manipulation of analogous material in this field would be generated in a similar manner to those concerned with the appropriate use of language.

NON-LINGUISTIC ANALOGUES

The next experiment (O'Connor and Hermelin, 1965) is concerned with non-verbal operations which, though not true analogies of linguistic processes, may nevertheless have some relevance. Similar operations to those which we investigated may play a part in the underlying cognitive structures of language development. These operations include those of ordering or seriation, cross-modal coding, immediate memory and cue-matching ability.

The relevance of ordering to language is an obvious one. Words are arranged in sentences and a sentence is the arrangement of words in a certain order. The problem of serial order in behaviour was first discussed by Lashley (1951) who pointed out that the association between words in sentences was not sufficient to account for grammatical structure. The argument stated that in addition to association between elements, one must also assume the existence of patterns and structural relationships. One relevant line of research has been concerned with this aspect of language. Using statistical approximations to English, it investigated the ability of people to supply appropriate words following series of different lengths. Accordingly a zero-order approximation consists of randomly selected words from a dictionary. In a first-order approximation, one word is supplied so that there is some measure of constraint in the selection of the next one. Higher-order approximations increasingly resemble normal spoken or written English. Experiments using such different language samples have demonstrated that higher-order approximations are easier learned and remembered, or perceived at a lower threshold of intensity, or against a higher level of background noise than are lower-order approximations.

The concept of seriation, as used by Inhelder and Piaget (1964) does, of course, imply more than the simple ordering of elements. Piaget argues that seriation is only possible when the child has reached a level of mental development at which he is able to carry out reversible operations. In this context this means that any element in a series can be classified in two ways, i.e. in a series of items of graded sizes, each item except the two extremes is smaller than some and larger than other items in the series. Thus the construction of a true series requires bi-directional comparisons to be made.

The relevance of the second operation to be investigated, i.e. cross-modal coding, is an obvious one. Language itself is in part a coding operation, in which something (a word or a sentence) stands for something else (an object, action, event, etc.) It is cross modal in so far as something heard is made equivalent to something seen, or something said to something done. Words act as signs and stand for the things they signify.

The role of memory in language is also clear. It is needed in the process of learning to speak, as illustrated by Brown (1965), who states that the number of words in spontaneously uttered sentences of young children closely matches their memory span. It is also essential in following the speech of others. Indeed, language and memory seem to be so closely connected that even with non-verbal material recall errors are based on acoustic confusion (Conrad, 1964).

The analogy between cue matching and the linguistic process, on the other hand, is perhaps somewhat more dubious. What we had in mind was the matching of similar elements in different contexts. Recognition of the identity of a display against various different backgrounds may be somewhat similar to recognizing a word as identical with the same word in a different context, except that phonologically probably no two repetitions of the same word are ever identical. However, as already mentioned, we would not claim a close analogy between any of the tasks we presented to our subjects in the following experiment, and operations involved in language processes. The experiment should be merely regarded as an attempt to investigate various complex functions on a non-verbal level.

We compared speaking and non-speaking autistic with subnormal and normal children on four perceptual–motor tasks, which included seriation, cross-modal coding, immediate memory and cue matching, (O'Connor and Hermelin, 1965a). The non-speaking autistic children did not understand language other than a very few simple words and commands. They were unable to obtain the minimum score of 2 years on a verbal comprehension test (Peabody Picture Vocabulary) in which the child has to point to one of four pictured objects named by the experimenter. They were thus assigned a verbal age of 1 year 9 months. The mean scores of the groups in terms of verbal comprehension age, as well as the mental age levels on a perceptual motor test (Seguin formboard) are given in Table 9.

TABLE 9. MEAN CHRONOLOGICAL AGE AND PERFORMANCE AND VERBAL MENTAL
AGE FOR ALL GROUPS

	N	CA	Seguin formboard	Peabody
Non-speaking autistics	12	10–10	5–6	1–9
Speaking autistics	12	11–9	6–0	4–1
Imbeciles	12	10–5	5–10	4–2
Normals	12	5–2	—	—

As children with very limited verbal comprehension took part in the experiment, no verbal instructions were given; the tasks and their solution were repeatedly demonstrated by the experimenter, and the child was then invited to repeat the demonstration. All successful performances were rewarded by sweets. The unsuccessful attempts at solutions were corrected.

The material used for all tasks consisted of cut-out red cardboard squares of various sizes. In the seriation task there were five such squares, the largest having an area of 400 square centimetres and the smallest 61 square centimetres. The experimenter set these out in a row, starting with the largest and finishing with the smallest. The squares were then taken up and given to the subject for reproduction of the arrangement. Twenty trials were allowed, each incorrect attempt being corrected. The cross-modal coding task required the subjects to determine which of two squares, one larger, one smaller, concealed a sweet. Two taps on the subjects' back signalled that the sweet was under the smaller; one tap that it was under the larger square. The third task was concerned with immediate memory. The subject was simultaneously shown two differently sized squares and had to select the one which immediately prior had been exposed for one second. Finally, for the last task on cue matching, two square cards of equal size, lightly hatched over with black diagonal lines, were presented. On one a large and on the other a small square was drawn. A third card, matching in size either the smaller or larger of the squares, was simultaneously presented, and the subject had to match this with the appropriate cue card. Twenty trials were allowed for each task.

An analysis of variance on the number of correctly performed trials on each task resulted in a significant groups-by-task interaction. Subsequent testing for simple effects showed the non-speaking autistic children performing at a chance level on all tasks. None of the autistic children did obtain above chance scores on the seriation tasks. On the cross-modal coding task, the autistic as well as the subnormal groups had chance results, and only the normals performed somewhat better. Normal, subnormal and speaking autistic children did equally well, and significantly better than the non-speaking autistic group on the memory tasks, while the speaking autistic and subnormal children both got similar scores on the cue matching test, which fall midway between those obtained by normals and non-speaking autistic children. These results are illustrated in Fig. 7.

Thus only the normal children scored above chance on the cross-modal coding task, although even they performed on a lower level on this than on the other tests. Normals and subnormals obtained high scores on

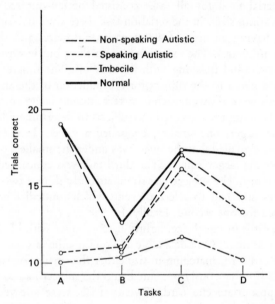

FIG. 7. Mean scores for four groups of subjects on the seriation (A), cross-modal coding (B), immediate memory (C) and cue matching tasks (D).

seriation, while both autistic groups, speaking and non-speaking, performed very badly. The immediate memory and cue-matching tests seem to be speech-dependent, as only the non-speaking children were unable to score above-chance level.

Several factors may be responsible for the failure of the autistic children to perform the seriation task. These include the number of items, the degree of difference between them, and the nature of the material. The complexity of a function such as ordering is demonstrated by the fact that the next experiment gave somewhat different results. In this experiment (O'Connor and Hermelin, 1967b) a semantically ordered sequence was used. For this the operation of "seriation" as used by Piaget, is not relevant, as reversability is not a feature of this series. On the contrary, the sequences in this experiment are unidirectional.

Twelve speaking autistic children with CAs between 7–4 and 15–8, mean CA 11–9, were compared with normals aged from 3–6 months to 5 years. The groups were individually matched with each other for verbal digit span. They were presented with visual tasks under four conditions. In all tasks four pictures, drawn on cards, were put in front of the child in a prearranged order. The child was allowed to look at these cards for 10 seconds. They were then removed, given to him, and he was asked to put them out again in the same order as before. In one instance the pictures were of four unconnected items, in another of two pairs of objects which followed each other in logical sequence, in a third, two random items were followed by a sequential pair and in the fourth test, a pair was followed by two random items. The material is illustrated in Fig. 8.

An analysis of the results showed that though the autistic children made somewhat more mistakes than the normals, they nevertheless did much better with pictures which had a predetermined order than with random ones. Thus in this experiment, speaking autistic children used a meaningful order as an aid for memory in a similar way as did normal controls. In this experiment, as in others concerned with visual memory in normals, no serial position effects were found. This was true of the autistic, as well as of the normal children. Immediate recall in the auditory–vocal modality, on the other hand, produce such effects, resulting in better recall of the last few of a series of items. We therefore asked whether categorization or recency would be more effective in determining which items would be recalled by autistic and normal children, if the series was presented auditorialy.

ORDERING AND IMMEDIATE MEMORY

We have already mentioned that one of the outstanding characteristics in the performance of autistic children is their good rote memory, which is evident in their echolalia. Echolalia is also found in many subnormal children, who may tend to repeat the last words being said to them. In

FIG. 8. Examples of pictures used in picture sequence experiment.

addition, the autistic child's speech shows delayed echolalic features. The child will store phrases said to him, and repeat them on another occasion. Goldfarb (1961) stated that his autistic children could only repeat language but could not understand it. Kanner (1946), in his first description of autistic speech, stressed this feature, and Rutter (1966) confirmed it in a more recent investigation. Rutter also found that the autistic children did better on tests of auditory rote memory than on any other, a finding which was repeated by Tubbs (1966). Tubbs also found no difference on immediate visual memory tests between autistic children and normal children of similar mental ages. O'Connor and Hermelin (1965a) in the experiment just reported, found no difference between their control groups and speaking autistic children in immediate visual memory. Even the non-speaking ones performed somewhat better on the memory tasks than on any of the other tests, though in their case, this was a statistically non-significant tendency.

With normals, immediate memory for verbal material is better for grammatically structured than unstructured messages, (Epstein et al., 1963; Marks and Miller, 1964) for conceptually similar than diverse material (Deese, 1961), and for higher than lower approximations to English. Better results are also obtained with frequent than with infrequent words and with word pairs of higher than lower association value. The improved scores to be found for patterned or structured messages might not be due to any improvement in the memory storage system, but may be attributable to successful guessing and predicting on the basis of one's knowledge of the characteristics of the language. Chomsky's argument that all grammatically transformed sentences seem to be generated spontaneously from a relatively small number of strings of underlying kernel sentences also had its influence on the view of psychologists. Lenneberg (1967) has argued that from the very beginning of speech general principles of semantic and syntatic operations are manifest. Miller (1964) also stresses that children must be naturally endowed with a strong predisposition for language learning, and that syntactic and semantic habits must have a productive quality. Such a biologically oriented point of view of language development could account for the language deficits and peculiarities in the autistic child not only in terms of an acquired cognitive disability, but in relation to some biologically or physiologically based maldevelopment.

In the experiment which has been reported, even speaking autistic children were found to be unable to order a reversible series, but could use a visually presented semantic sequence. The next question we asked was whether such ordering or seriation was in any way comparable with the ordering of words in the construction of sentences. The following experiment (Hermelin and O'Connor, 1967b), investigated the relationship between immediate verbal recall with word frequency, sequential probability and conceptual organization in twelve subnormal and twelve speaking autistic children. The subjects were aged between 8 years and 14 years 5 months, with a mean age of 10 years 8 months. They were matched on the Peabody Vocabulary Test, which requires the visual recognition of spoken words. Mental ages on this test ranged from 2 years 6 months to 10 years 8 months, mean 4 years 3 months. The subjects were also matched individually on their immediate auditory-vocal memory span for digits, which ranged from 2 to 7, with a mean span of 4.5 digits.

The material we used were one-syllable words, selected from a vocabulary list for subnormals (Mein, 1961). This list contains 1720 words and their frequency of occurrence in the speech of a sample of eighty cases.

The selected words were presented in messages of four words each. Sixteen of these four-word messages were matched for frequency. Four consisted of simple English sentences (A), and four others contained the same words as the whole of the first set, but with the words occurring in random order (A1). These two arrangements were repeated with other words in two further sets, one of sentence (B) and one of random word sequences (B1). Alternate subjects were presented with sentences and random arrangements from these different sets, so that one subject heard set A and B1, and the next had to recall set B and A1. In addition, there was also a set of four sentences of infrequent words (C) which all subjects had to recall. Thus, two different comparisons of recall scores could be made. In one the effect of word frequency could be compared. In the other, we compared recall of sentences and random arrangements of words of matched frequency. Examples of the material are given in Table 10.

The messages were presented vocally at the rate of two words per second. The order in which frequent sentences, random words, and infrequent sentence material was presented to each subject was determined by a balanced design. Recall after each message was immediate, but the rate of recall itself had to be unpaced. Though all children could be persuaded to try and repeat as many words as they remembered, it was not possible for them to do this at a fixed rate. Every effort was made consistent with a co-operative and optimal performance by the child, to ensure that his rate of recall was similar to that of other subjects and relatively constant.

TABLE 10. EXAMPLES OF MATERIAL

Frequent word sentences (A)	Frequent word sentences (B)
We went to town	*What is the time*
Frequent random words (A1)	Frequent random words (B1)
Some that a went	*Light what leaf the*
Infrequent word sentences (C)	
Shade this young plant	

The results of this recall experiment were scored in terms of number of messages correct. A correct message was one in which all words were repeated in the correct order. These scores were then treated by analysis of variance. When sentences containing infrequent words were compared with random arrangements of frequent words, the recall scores did not differ significantly, even for the subnormal children. Thus word frequency and grammatical structure could be regarded as factors giving equivalent results in these experiments. Though these types of material did not result in a significant conditions term in these comparisons, the group terms was highly significant. The autistic children had higher recall scores, i.e. remembered better, than the subnormal controls.

A further comparison was made between scores obtained for the recall of sentences containing frequent words, and words of the same frequency presented in a random order. In this comparison, the result was a highly significant groups-by-conditions interaction. This showed that the subnormal children did much better with sentences than with unconnected words. This difference between the two kinds of material affected the recall of the autistic children far less. In fact, for them the difference between their recall scores for sentences and random word arrangements was not statistically significant.

Thus this experiment provided us with two results. The first was a confirmation of previous observations that autistic children have auditory–verbal immediate memories, which are at least as good as those of sub-normals of similar mental development. The second one was that when words matched for frequency were presented in the form of sentences, they were easier for subnormal children to recall, than when they were presented in random order. This, however, did not apply to the same extent to the autistic children. If the greater ease with which meaning-fully organized material is remembered is due to the subject's ability to predict the items on the basis of his previous knowledge of the nature of the order in which they are organized, then it follows that the autistic child fails to make use of such an order because he does not recognize it.

Reliance on an "echobox" type memory store (Craik, 1966) for audi-tory–vocal recall would result in favouring the most recent or last item in a series to be recalled. If on the other hand a classified storage system were used, structured material would determine recall more than recency. The following experiment (O'Connor and Hermelin, 1967b) tested this assumption. Thirty-six children acted as subjects. There were twenty-four normals, twelve of them aged 4 years 11 months to 5 years, and twelve aged 3 years 6 months to 4 years 8 months. Twelve speaking autistic children were aged between 7 years 4 months and 15 years 8 months, mean 11 years 9 months. All subjects were individually matched for memory span for digits across groups, and the verbal sequences used for the experimental procedure were twice the subject's individual memory span in all cases.

The words in the passages to be presented for recall were selected from the Mein and O'Connor (1960) vocabulary, and had frequencies between 30 and 90 per cent. All messages were matched for an average word fre-quency of 50 per cent. Each child was presented with four examples for each of four types of message. Order of presentation of conditions was balanced and randomized between subjects. Presentation rate was at the speed of two words per second, and recall was immediate and unpaced.

It can be seen from the material illustrated in Table 11 that in one condition randomly arranged words have to be recalled, while in another it is two short sentences of equal length. In the remaining conditions a random arrangement of words is followed by a sentence of equal length, or, conversely, randomly arranged words follow a sentence. The results

TABLE 11. EXAMPLES OF EIGHT-WORD MESSAGES

Random–random

| day | she | farm | when; cat | fall | back | rake |

Random–sentence

| wall | long | cake | sand; where | is | the | ship? |

Sentence–random

| read | them | your | book; way | spoon | here | like |

Sentence–sentence

| ride | home | by | car; write | to | us | now |

were scored separately for the first and second half of each message, so that the number of words correctly recalled for first or second half as well as from sentences or random arrangements could be compared. The results of these comparisons are illustrated in Fig. 9.

An analysis of variance of the recall scores resulted in two highly significant interaction terms, i.e. groups by positions and groups by conditions. The first of these confirmed that though all groups showed the effect of recency on recall, this was far more marked in the autistic children than in the normal groups. The second interaction illustrated, that though sentences were recalled better than random arrangements by all subjects, this effect was much more marked in the normal than in the autistic children. Recall scores for randomly arranged words were the same for all groups, while sentences were significantly better recalled by the normal than by the autistic children. This difference between random and non-random arrangements was more marked in the older than in the younger normal children.

Similar results to those were obtained by Maccoby (1967) in a selective listening experiment. Children of various ages had to repeat words spoken by either a male or female voice, when these were simultaneously heard. Sequential probability of the messages was varied, and it was found that the degree of such sequential probability in either the target or the matching voice did not affect the recall scores of the youngest children. Older children performed significantly better when the message was sequentially highly probable than when it was not. The results were explained in terms of the older children having greater familiarity with probable sequences between words, being in a better position to fill in poorly heard sequences of a message on the basis of the context in which the ambiguous segment occurs.

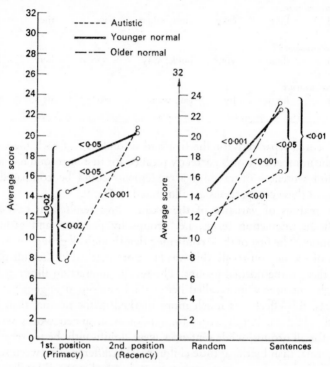

FIG. 9. Auditory recall for random words and sentences in autistic and younger and older normal children.

MEMORY AND MEANING

Though grammar and meaning are not totally independent, these variables can be manipulated independently, as in the experiments by Miller and Isard (1963) and Marks and Miller (1964). The results from these experiments indicate that for adults meaningful grammatical sentences are easiest to hear against background noise, and are also easiest to remember. Semantically and grammatically anomalous word strings are equally difficult, and it seems from this that comprehension and memory depend on meaning and syntax to about the same extent. Random strings of words were by far the most difficult to perceive and recall. McNeil (1965) repeated the experiment with children aged between 5 and 8 years, and found that by the age of 8, children also do significantly better with meaningful and grammatical sentences. As in Marks and Miller's experiment, there seemed to be no significant difference between efficiency in dealing with semantically or grammatically anomalous material.

Some experiments do demonstrate that grammar may override meaning in determining ease of learning or level of recall. Epstein (1961, 1962) showed that nonsense syllables, resembling grammatical English in endings and structural arrangement, were learned faster than randomly arranged meaningful words. On the other hand, meaning can be elicited from word arrangements in the absence of recognizable grammatical structure, as is illustrated by much modern prose writing and poetry. The meaning in those cases is often arrived at by the conceptual associations underlying the words. More conventional forms of association were used in experiments by Bousfield (1953) and Deese (1961). In these experiments, the subjects were presented with a randomly arranged series of words falling into a limited number of conceptual categories. In recall tests related items tended to be recalled together in clusters, and the amount of such clustering was positively correlated with the amount recalled. Comparable results concerned with sensory channelling have been reported by Broadbent (1958). According to Broadbent's theoretical model, related material is passed through a filter into a memory store, while other material is held in a prior short-term store for subsequent processing. The results from the clustering experiments could also be accounted for by selective filtering, which deals with the incoming stimuli according to their common characteristics.

Our next experiment (Hermelin and O'Connor, 1967b), attempted to investigate whether not only the appreciation of grammatical structure, but also semantic association processes, as shown by "clustering" were impaired in autistic children. The subjects were matched for auditory memory span. There were twelve children in each group. The mean age of the autistic and subnormal children was 10 years 8 months, and the mean age of the normals 4 years 3 months. The word sequences which were presented for recall were eight words long, which was beyond the immediate memory span for any of the subjects. They consisted of one message for control purposes, and three others, which could be meaningfully clustered. Each message was spoken at the rate of two words per second, and recall was immediate and unpaced. The order of messages presented was varied and balanced between subjects. The messages are given in Table 12.

TABLE 12. MATERIAL FOR CLUSTERING EXPERIMENT

(1)	Blue	three	red	five	six	white	green	eight
(2)	Nine	this	one	tea	four	is	ten	cold
(3)	Glass	hand	cow	pot	cup	meat	spoon	place
(4)	Ship	gun	night	home	jug	time	lamp	farm

It will be seen that the first message contains colour and number words. The second consists of a short sentence with digits interpolated between its words. In sequence 3, names of table utensils were presented together with interpolated random words. Sequence 4 served as a control condition and contained randomly selected words. Reordering of items into related clusters was significantly more frequent in the normal and subnormal than in the autistic children, and occurred with the same frequency for the three messages.

These results suggest that autistic children are not only impaired in the appreciation of the grammatically structured aspects of language, but that they also lack an ability to associate words semantically. Their recall ability for words may depend largely on the purely acoustic and phonetic aspects of speech.

RECALL AND PHONIC EMPHASIS

Brown and Fraser (1963) have shown that children who learn to speak show consistent structural peculiarities in their speech. They reduce English sentences in a meaningful, systematic manner, producing something like "telegraphic English" and retaining keywords which give maximal information, while omitting the connecting words. This selection may be the result of a communication analysis, since the words retained carry most of the information, while those omitted are largely predictable from the context. On the other hand, keywords may be retained simply because they usually receive more emphasis in the speech of adults. It may be that the intricate combination of key and emphasized words influence the appreciation of meaningful structure. Miller and Chomsky (1963) point out the distinction between the syntactic and phonological factors, and their relationship to meaning. In this context the role of key-words would be a part of the syntactic structure, while the phonic component would be represented through emphasis. Miller and Chomsky see the syntactic component of language as a set of rules for analysing word sequences and formulating new utterances, whereas the phonological component consists of processes which give shape to an utterance in acoustic articulatory terms. Clinical observations have suggested that in addition to semantic and syntactic abnormalities, autistic children often show deviations from normal phonological speech patterns (Goldfarb *et al.*, 1956). These include insufficiency as well as incorrectness of stress, volume, pitch and intonation which results in such peculiar qualities of speech as whisper, sing-song, flatness of voice, or the speech apparently resembling different voices on different occasions. In collaboration with us Frith (1969) has carried out a study to investigate whether syntactic or phonological structure affects immediate recall in autistic children.

Thirty-two children acted as subjects. Sixteen normal children were drawn from a nursery school, and had a mean CA of 4 years 3 months. The autistic children all had some speech, and were selected according to the criteria previously described. Their mean CA was 11 years 6 months, ranging from 7 years 8 months to 16 years 1 month. The groups were matched according to their digit span. Digit span increases with development, and Jensen (1964) has suggested that it correlates highly with general intellectual level. Consequently one may assume that the groups were intellectually comparable. The groups were also matched for their comprehension of words, as tested by the Peabody Vocabulary test. The mean verbal mental age for the normals was 3 years 11 months, ranging from 2 years 5 months to 5 years 7 months. For the autistics, the mean was 4 years 9 months, ranging from 2 years 1 month to 10 years 5 months. The groups did not differ statistically in verbal mental age. The experimental tasks was the recall of spoken messages.

On the basis of the digit span, the subjects were subdivided into "low-span" groups with a span of 3 or 4 digits, and "high-span" groups with spans of 5, 6 or 7 digits. The same words were used to make up messages of two types: "sense" and "nonsense". "Sense" messages consisted of correct meaningful and syntactical structure. "Nonsense" sequences were words arranged in random order. Half of the "sense" and half of the "nonsense" lists were presented while stressing connecting words. This was termed "unnatural stress". The rest of the material was presented with stress on the keywords. "Stress" was defined as loudness, though Fry (1958) showed that factors such as pitch and duration may play a part as well. Each subject recalled forty-eight lists, sixteen consisting of four words, sixteen of six words and sixteen of eight words for the low span groups, and lists of ten, twelve and fourteen words for the subjects with a high digit span. Each group of sixteen lists contained four examples of "sense–natural stress", four of "sense–unnatural stress", four of "nonsense–natural stress", and four of "nonsense–unnatural stress". Examples of these word lists are given in Table 13. Words were presented at the rate of two per second. Stressed words were at an intensity level of 78–83 db, and

TABLE 13. EXAMPLES OF VERBAL MATERIAL IN PHONOLOGICAL
STRESS EXPERIMENT

1. Sense–natural stress: keywords stressed,
   connecting words unstressed in a sentence.
   "*Read* them your *book*".

2. Sense–unnatural stress: keywords unstressed, connecting
   words stressed in a sentence.
   "Get *off his* bed".

3. Nonsense–natural stress: keywords stressed,
   connecting words unstressed in a random list.
   "*Show* us was *house*".

4. Nonsense–unnatural stress: keywords unstressed,
   connecting words stressed in a random list.
   "*The* gave his *there*".

unstressed ones of 60–68 db. The recall scores were based on the number of words correctly recalled, regardless of order.

In order to compare high span and low span groups, percentage scores were used for analyses. A highly significant groups-by-conditions interaction was found, and further statistical testing gave the following results. Normals with higher spans showed significantly greater differences between sense and nonsense than any other group. Autistic children with higher span improved more under "sense" as compared with "nonsense" conditions than autistic children with lower span.

As far as the phonological aspects were concerned, normals with higher span showed significantly less difference between stress and non-stress than normal children with lower spans, who recalled stressed words much better than unstressed words. The same difference between autistic children with higher and lower spans approached but did not reach a statistically significant level.

Keywords were significantly affected by stress; they were better recalled when stressed than when not stressed. The effect of stress on connecting words was significantly less marked. There was an indication that subjects with lower digit span showed the effect of stress on connecting words more than those with higher spans.

These results provide some information additional to that previously discussed. Though the appreciation of grammatical structure increases with increasing digit span in the autistic group, autistic children with higher spans still remain less able to make use of structure than normals with matched spans. It seems that in autistic children this inability to make adequate use of syntactic structure in a meaningful context is part of some basic deficiency, additional to any existing low mental age. In contrast to this, the effects of phonological structure are equal for normal and autistic groups. All groups recall stressed keywords better than unstressed keywords, but recall is not different for stressed and unstressed connecting words. This is regardless of syntactical context, and implies that emphasis is as relevant for autistic as for normal children.

One might regard syntactic structure as intrinsic to a verbal pattern, transforming it into a sentence. On the other hand, at least in this experiment, phonological structure was provided externally by placing emphasis on certain words, though Chomsky has stressed the internally determined factors in interpreting intonation. It appears that autistic children are not retarded in the appreciation of these physical structure variables, as opposed to the internal structure variables of syntax. They make as much use of emphasis in recall as normals do. This finding is consistent with the hypothesis of an echobox type memory in the more retarded of the autistic children: the phonological qualities of language are preserved, since by definition such a store reflects physical acoustic properties of speech. These results show that autistic children are more influenced by the physical qualities of auditory stimuli than by their semantic or structural aspects, and should be related to findings from the previously mentioned study (O'Connor and Hermelin, 1967b). In this experiment which compared the effects of words and sounds, we found that the responses of autistic children were more affected by the position and intensity of the stimuli than by their qualitative differences, i.e. whether words or sounds were presented. These findings are confirmed by the results indicating the effectiveness of phonological stress and the relative lack of the effects of semantic and structural organization of verbal material.

SUMMARY

Experimenters concerned with impairment in language development must investigate possible deficits in the areas of semantics, grammar and phonology. The importance of the presence or absence of speech for other, non-linguistic operations, must also be considered. While all autistic children were unable to learn a seriation task, speaking children were better than non-speaking ones in cue matching and visual memory. Some of these problems were presented as non-linguistic analogues, and a similar technique is used in the ITPA, which tests linguistic operations in different sensory channels. Decoding (input analysis) and association (processing) was particularly impaired at the auditory-vocal, but less deficient in the visual–motor channels. Encoding processes (output) were grossly inadequate in all modalities tested.

While autistic children had been unable to perform a reversible seriation task, they could appreciate a semantically determined, unidirectional arrangement of pictures. On the other hand, in a recall test they failed to rearrange words into conceptual categories.

Findings indicating an intact auditory memory span in autistic children were confirmed by results from the ITPA and by scores from verbal recall experiments. Autistic children remembered at least as many randomly arranged words as did normals and subnormals. However, while recall performance for the controls improved drastically when sentences instead of random words had to be recalled, this difference was not significant for the autistic children. In a further study the effects of recency and sequential order were compared. While normal children always recalled sentences better than non-sentences, regardless of their serial position, this was not the case for autistic children. Recall scores showed strong recency effects, which were significantly more marked in determining recall than the qualitative characteristics of the verbal material. Thus, though auditory–verbal memory capacity is not impaired in autistic children, the recall process depends on an "echo-box type" memory store. Coding and categorizing processes are deficient, and "sense" is little better remembered than "nonsense". The results indicate a relative absence of a semantic as well as of a syntactical analysis.

In contrast to this, we found that phonological stress was as effective for autistic as for normal children in determining what items were recalled. This indication of a memory mechanism which depended largely on the retention of the physical qualities of verbal stimuli is confirmed in experiments in which autistic children made no response distinction in orientating towards words as compared with noise. They were more affected by the intensity than by the quality of auditory stimulation. Thus we found severe impairment in the areas of grammatical and semantic aspects of language in autistic children, but normal responses to the phonological components.

CHAPTER 4

RESPONSIVENESS
IN AUTISTIC CHILDREN

AROUSAL AND CHILDHOOD AUTISM

The degree and direction of responsiveness shown by an individual at any given time is a function of the stimuli, both internal and external, to which he is subjected. Input may be dealt with as specific information. It may also have a more general influence on the motivational and arousal state of the organism, which would be additional to the level of arousal which can exist independent of sensory input. Responses to stimulation are distinguished not only in terms of their generality or specificity, but according to whether they are brief or more sustained. All such responses can be measured on the physiological and on the behavioural level. Though these two indicators often correlate (Lindsley, 1958; Lansing et al., 1959), paradoxical reactions, in which a high level of physiological arousal is found, together with a low level of behavioural responsiveness, also occur (Hermelin and O'Connor, 1968; Venables, 1968).

On the physiological level, measures of arousal have included the lowering of sensory threshholds, dilation of pupils and increased muscle tension. These may, or may not, correspond to other indicators, such as increased heart rate and breathing. According to Sokolov (1958) an orienting reflex includes a contraction of blood vessels in the limbs, in contrast to those in the head, which dilate. Another autonomic measure of arousal is the degree of the electrical conductivity of the skin. In arousal reactions, or in arousal states, this increases because of increased activity of the sweat glands. A distinction must be made between basic levels of conductivity, and responses to stimuli which are super-imposed on these levels (Venables and Martin, 1967). On the cortical level, the occipital alpha rhythm of 8–13 cps present in the EEG when the subject is in a relaxed state, blocks in

92

response to stimulation, and the EEG becomes desynchronized. If the organism is drowsy, flat slow EEG recordings are obtained prior to stimulation, and alpha waves may appear subsequently. Specific evoked electrical responses may be obtained from the visual and somethetic areas of the brain, but a more general evoked potential in response to stimulation can also be obtained from the vertex of the head.

While in resting subjects the degree of autonomic activity, such as heart rate, or level of skin conductance tends to be negatively correlated with the level of EEG activity, in stimulated conditions autonomic and EEG activation generally occur together (Darrow et al., 1946; Darrow et al., 1942; Hadley, 1941). Differential response patterns for different stimulus modalities have also been established. Visual and tactile stimuli, for instance, evoke alpha blocking, and also lead to an increased amplitude in the skin conductance response. But with successive visual stimulation, skin conductance diminishes, and finally extinguishes completely, while alpha blocking persists. The reverse pattern occurs in response to repeated tactile stimulation where the alpha waves reappear, while the skin conductance responses persist (Sokolov, 1958). Such selective arousal patterns can be found not only in relation to different physiological systems, but also in relation to different sensory pathways. In their classical series of experiments, Hernandez-Peon and his colleagues (1956) have demonstrated that stimulation of different points in the reticular system of the cat will selectively block activity in sensory pathways, and Sharpless and Jasper (1956) demonstrated habituation of arousal responses. The earlier findings of Bernhaut et al. (1953) showing different arousal values for different stimulus modalities in animals have been confirmed with infants. In the new born, non-specific EEG responses are most readily evoked by somesthetic, followed by auditory and finally by visual stimulation (Ellingson, 1960). The responses are of vertex origin and decrease in amplitude as stimulus intensity decreases (Ellingson, 1964; Barnett and Goodwin, 1965). Specific cortical visually evoked responses also occur in the newborn (Dustman and Beck, 1966; Ferris et al., 1966; Ellingson, 1966). No investigations on auditory or somesthetic evoked responses in infants seem to have been reported.

Sokolov (1958), differentiating between general and specific arousal, attributes the first to lower brain stem sections of the reticular formation, and the second to the thalamic region, which seems able to activate

P.E.A.C.—D*

cortical areas separately. He follows Sherrington (1960) who distinguished between phasic and tonic skeletal reflexes, by extending these concepts to orientating responses. Phasic orientation is specific and short lasting, and follows the onset, termination or change of a stimulus. This component is the one usually called the orientating reaction. Tonic orientation is more gradual, persists longer and is more general, i.e. it is a general arousal response. Psychologists such as Hutt *et al.* (1964) or Schopler (1965) who use the concept of arousal in relation to the behaviour of autistic children, have not always specified whether they were concerned with the general or specific aspect of the process. The same criticism can be applied to the indiscriminate use of psychological terms such as for instance, "attention" to describe general as well as specifically selected responses to stimuli. As Berlyne (1958) has pointed out, the concept of attention has probably had a more varied usage than perhaps any other in psychology. Like the term "arousal", it has been referred to in describing the degree of general alertness or vigilance, as well as the process that determines which aspect of a stimulus field will be selected as relevant for a set of responses. Though these are logically two quite distinct functions, they may nevertheless share some aspects of a common mechanism.

Several investigators have attempted to account for the abnormalities of behaviour found in autistic children in terms of a disfunction of the arousal mechanisms. Perhaps the most detailed account in theoretical terms is that of Rimland (1964). However, Rimland's (1964) theory, regarding the reticular formation as responsible for the linking of perception and memory, is too speculative and general to make a detailed discussion of it profitable. It involves the assumption that ". . . the reticular formation is the site at which sensory input (and perhaps also imaginal input) represented as highly complex electrical patterns, is integrated and converted to a code which makes it compatible with the retrieval system used in making available a wide range of the content of memory". It is due to disturbance of this process which, according to Rimland, may lead to the abnormalities of behaviour in childhood autism. It is to Rimland's credit that he states that most neuro-physiologists, e.g. Jasper (1954) would be sceptical about such a view of the functioning of the reticular formation.

Hutt *et al.* (1964) note several points which suggest to them that autistic children "are in a chronically high state of arousal". These are (1) resting

EEG records with a predominance of low voltage, fast, desynchronized waves; (2) behavioural withdrawal and stereotyped behaviour which are both associated with states of high arousal in animals, (3) increase in stereotyped behaviour with increasing environmental stimulation; (4) decrease in stereotyping and increasing synchronization of the EEG in an empty room; (5) high thresholds for pain and auditory stimuli, which is attributable to a possible blocking of sensory pathways, and (6) striving by the children to maintain "sameness".

Schopler (1965) attributes receptor deficiencies in autistic children to "sensory deprivation which results from an interaction between a constitutional deficiency, inhibiting certain reticular arousal functions and mothering tending to understimulate". The validity of this interpretation does not appear to have been tested.

We have already described our results (Hermelin and O'Connor, 1964; O'Connor and Hermelin, 1965b), concerned with the hierarchical organization of responses to stimuli in different modalities. To relate such response preferences to their differential arousal functions would seem somewhat tenuous, and moreover, the generality of the concepts makes interpretation ambiguous. Did the autistic children refrain from responding to sound because they were not aroused by it? Or did they fail to respond because their own level of arousal was already so high that they tended to ignore those stimuli which would most increase arousal? How would results such as those which showed an increase of response frequency with increased intensity of the stimulus fit into the overarousal hypothesis? Another question to be considered in this context is the relevance of the arousal hypothesis for social withdrawal. Venables (1968) reports a number of experiments which show positive correlations between the degree of autonomic and cortical responsiveness and the degree of social withdrawal in non-paranoid chronic schizophrenic adults. Venables concludes that there is evidence that the more withdrawn these patients are, the higher their cortical and subcortical arousal level. Though Hutt et al. (1964) do not refer to Venables, their conclusions are based on similar arguments, although in their investigations the evidence is far less definitive.

RESPONSES TO INTERNAL AND EXTERNAL STIMULI

To test the degree of response which a stimulus evokes, the influence of other background stimuli is reduced to a minimum, while the stimulus to which response behaviour is to be tested is made to stand out. In our first studies of responsiveness (Hermelin and O'Connor, 1963), we noted the amount of approach to, and the orientation towards, various stimuli in autistic children and subnormal controls. Mayer-Gross et al. (1955) have described such children as being "independent of and unresponsive to the environment". We asked ourselves whether such unresponsiveness, if indeed it existed, was selective rather than general, and whether it was more marked in one kind of environment than in another. We were also interested in the degree to which behaviour of a stereotyped kind, which was apparently not in response to environmental stimuli, would nevertheless be under environmental control.

We selected twelve autistic children, all resident in an institution for mentally subnormal children. They were aged from 5 to 16 years, mean age 9 years. Though five out of the twelve were judged by psychiatrists to possess "islands of normal or near normal intellectual function against a background of serious retardation" (Creak, 1961), all subjects functioned on a severely subnormal level. Five children were without speech, and speech in the others was grossly retarded. The autistic children were matched for sex, age and IQ with a subnormal group from the same hospital, who were judged by the psychiatrist as free of autistic symptoms, such as outlined by Creak et al. (1961), except for retardation of speech. Case records noted a number of abnormalities in both groups, which are shown in Table 14.

Each child took part in six sessions of 15 minutes each. They were put individually into a large empty room and observed through a one-way screen. The first session served as an accommodation period, to get the child used to the situation and the surroundings. The second session, again in the empty room, provided base line observations in regard to motility, vocalization and orientation towards the room fixtures, i.e. doors, windows and light switches. Each one of a list of items of behaviour occurring within a period of 1 minute was given a score of 1. Of course, many forms of behaviour occurred within each 1-minute period, and were scored for this time period, but the maximum score for any one item in any one session of 15 minutes was 15. The list of items is given in Table 14.

TABLE 14. LIST OF ACTIVITIES SCORED

1. Smiling	12. Lying down (sitting)
2. Crying	13. Covering eyes or ears
3. Vocalizing	14. Looking at pictures
4. Grimacing	15. Turning towards voice
5. Rocking	16. Playing with toys
6. Twisting	17. Approaching person
7. Finger play	18. Retreating from or ignoring person
8. Door	19. Responding to person (non-verbal)
9. Windows	20. Carrying out verbal commands
10. Light switches	21. Talking to experimenter
11. Walking about (running)	

After the second 15-minute period in the empty room, three pictures were put on three separate walls for the next session. These included a plain red paper, an abstract pattern and a representational picture of people and animals. At the fourth session auditory stimuli were substituted. Loudspeakers on the walls emitted nursery tunes or white noise, at an intensity of 70 db. In the fifth session, manipulative stimuli were provided, i.e. a puzzle, a spinning top and a piece of string. Finally, in the sixth session one of the experimenters entered the room and attempted to engage the child in social communication. This last session will be described in detail in its appropriate context. For the moment, we will only deal with the other modes of stimulation.

Analysis of variance compared the frequency of discrete orienting responses elicited by the visual, auditory and manipulative stimuli, as well as by the fixtures of the room, with apparently non-directed behaviour, which we termed "self-generated". Figure 10 illustrates the frequency of these two behaviour categories over the six sessions.

"Self-generated" behaviour (which consisted mainly of random motor movement, including rocking, hand and finger play and spinning) did not vary from session to session, but the autistic groups scored higher on these items than the control group. Conversely, in the response behaviour

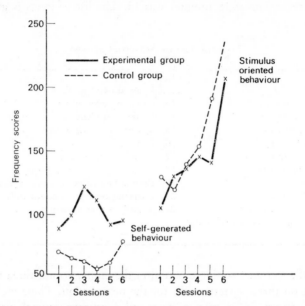

Fig. 10. Mean frequency scores for autistic and subnormal children.

category there were significant differences between sessions but not between groups, except during the period in which manipulative stimuli were provided. These were more often ignored by the autistic children than by the controls. It will be remembered that Wing (1967) describing another group of autistic children, found that what most distinguished them from other variously impaired control groups and from normals was the autistic children's lack of play. On the other hand, in this experiment, visual and auditory stimuli elicited the same amount of orienting behaviour in the autistic children as they did in the controls.

"Self-generated" behaviour might be thought to interfere with responses to external stimuli. However, response behaviour varied between different stimulus conditions, while self-generated behaviour did not. Thus the two forms of activity must be regarded as relatively independent of each other.

Similar variables to those just described were used in the following experiment (O'Connor and Hermelin, 1963b), using different groups of hospitalized autistic and subnormal children. The clinical characteristics of the groups were similar to those previously tested, and are given in Table 15.

There were twelve autistic and twelve subnormal children in this study, aged between 9 and 16 years; IQs were matched, ranging from 20 to 58 points on the Wechsler Adult Scale. In this experiment, the children were individually presented with a series of displays. These included a large cardboard box, a rocking platform, a blanket, the sound of a voice heard through a loudspeaker, a model of a woman and finally the presence of one of the experimenters. All displays were visual except one, and in all the visual instances tactual exploration of the display was possible. Data from two sources was recorded: the distance of the child from the stimulus object at any given moment, and the amount of movement of the child. These data were recorded in the following manner: at increasing distances from the display, three lights shining on three photoelectric cells let into the skirting board, activated pens on a recorder in an adjoining room. Whenever a subject crossed the floor between a light and the photocell on the opposite wall, the light beam was interrupted, and this interruption was marked on the recorder. Thus the subject's position in the room was noted continuously. Distance from the stimulus object was scored as time spent in any one of four parts of the room during a 5-minute period. Motility was scored simply by the addition of the number of times the child crossed the light beam. Analyses of variance showed that autistic children remained more distant from the box, the rocking platform and the blanket than did the controls. They spent as much time as the subnormal children near the loud speaker, the model of the woman, and the experimenter. These latter findings will be discussed in more detail in the context of the social behaviour of autistic children. For the present, it is worth noting that the children tended to approach the three "non-social" stimulus objects, i.e. the box, the rocking platform and the blanket, rather less than did the subnormals. This could be attributed to the difference between the motility scores, which were significantly higher for the autistic than for the control groups. In other words, when the autistic children approached the objects, they went as near to them as the subnormals, but the latter tended to spend longer times in close proximity to these stimuli, while the autistic children spent more time moving about the room. It is of some interest that for all subjects a highly significant

TABLE 15. INCIDENCE OF RELEVANT CLINICAL SIGNS

Groups	Hospitals	Complications of pregnancy and delivery toxaemia, etc.	Encephalitis and meningitis	Epilepsy	Strabismus	Overt neurological disease
Autistic (N = 24)	1	4	3	3	3	1
	2	7	0	1	4	3
		11	3	4	7	4
Control (N = 24)	1	7	0	0	4	2
	2	0	0	3	0	1
		7	0	3	4	3

negative correlation between IQ and amount of motility was found. The most active children had the lowest IQs.

These two studies measuring the amount of responses elicited by various stimuli, tended to show that if orienting behaviour was measured as in the first study (Hermelin and O'Connor, 1963), there was no difference between the groups. However, when continuous instead of discrete observations were made, as in the second experiment (O'Connor and Hermelin, 1963b) when a running record was kept, responses were less sustained in the autistic children. This latter finding was repeated in the eye movement study which has already been described (O'Connor and Hermelin, 1967a). When total inspection time of visual stimuli was measured, autistic children had lower scores than the controls. However, when the number of eye fixations, regardless of length of such fixations, were scored, this was not significantly different between autistic and subnormal children.

There is thus an indication in our results that the orienting component in response to stimulation does not differ substantially from that of subnormals. On the other hand, there seems to be faster adaptation in autistic children. Interest in various stimuli seems to be aroused for a shorter time than in normals or subnormals. Schopler's results (1966) about the shorter time spent by autistic children with visually presented stimuli, confirm this finding. However, he also found that the youngest of his normal control group (age 5–7) had visual inspection times as brief as those of the autistic children, whereas we find that normal children of the same age as his group, or even younger, looked longer at visual stimuli than did the autistic children. While Schopler found no significant difference in time spent in tactual exploration by autistic, normal and subnormal children, Hutt et al. (1965) do report such differences in the manipulative as well as in the visual modality, confirming our results of significantly less manipulation of toys by autistic children than by subnormal controls (Hermelin and O'Connor, 1963).

ATTENTION AND ADAPTATION

The amount of response to novelty has also been used as an indication for the degree of arousal. Berlyne (1960) defines novelty as either "absolute" or "relative". In the former case, the properties in a stimulus will never have been encountered before by the organism. The latter describes stimuli in which familiar elements or qualities are combined into patterns which the organism has not experienced before. Additionally, Berlyne distinguishes between "long term" and "short term" novelty. A stimulus has properties of "long term" novelty when it has not been encountered for periods of days, months or years, and "short term" novelty when it has not been perceived for a period of seconds, minutes or hours. Direct evidence for novelty as one of the stimulus properties determining attention and arousal comes from an experiment by Sharpless and Jasper (1956). They recorded the EEG in cats with inserted needle electrodes, following the presentation of loud sounds. The sounds lasted for about three seconds and were presented at irregular intervals while the cats were asleep. At first the sounds evoked bursts of irregular high frequency waves. With succeeding stimuli this arousal reaction tended to become shorter and shorter until it finally disappeared. There is thus a clear connection between arousal and novelty, but it does not follow that lack of response to novel stimulation is always due to a pre-existing high arousal state, leading to the avoidance of further arousal.

Another factor which must be borne in mind is the role played by development in response to change. Löwenfeld (1927) and Bühler et al. (1928) have shown that the first reaction of infants to the unfamiliar is frequently one of displeasure and rejection. Only as the child matures does he begin to show positive responses to novel stimuli. The observations about the insistence on sameness were made on autistic children aged 2–6 years in the Hutt et al. (1965) study. If one takes into account that the mental age of the children might have been considerably lower than the chronological ages, the rejection of novelty could possibly be regarded as a developmental effect, due to low mental age rather than high level of arousal. This interpretation seems to be supported by an experiment by Spitz and Hoats (1961) who showed that novelty was not a very potent factor in determining responses in retarded children. Cantor (1963) found that normal kindergarten children spend more time in selecting and viewing novel rather than familiar visual stimuli, and Berlyne (1960) obtained similar findings from normal adults. He presented subjects with pairs of pictures of animals for 10 seconds. For ten trials one animal reappeared constantly on one or the other side, paired each time with a picture of a new, different animal. It was found that subjects spend more and more of the 10 seconds fixating the novel picture. Novelty in such a procedure would be defined as relative and short term.

The preference shown by autistic children for sameness has been regarded by Kanner (1943) as highly characteristic of the syndrome. Creak et al. (1961) also note "resistance to change" as typical behaviour of autistic children. It will be necessary to investigate in this context the two dimensions of novelty mentioned by Berlyne (1960), i.e. the degree of novelty and the time intervals between presentations. One might question whether these variables measure the same dimensions as are used by clinicians in concept such as the "insistence on sameness" and "resistance to change". None the less, it seemed of interest whether those clinical observations could be extended to include visual inspection of a relatively familiar rather than a relatively novel picture by autistic children. For this experiment, the same subjects and apparatus as described previously (O'Connor and Hermelin, 1967a) were used. Autistic, subnormal and normal children took part. The first two groups were aged between 6 and 16, with IQs between 25 and 75. The normals were matched for chronological age with the mental age of the subnormals, which ranged from 3 years to 6 years.

The apparatus was the same wooden box described earlier. The child could look in through an opening, where he could see two display cards, one at an angle of 35° to the right, and the other at 35° to the left of the midline. Only the cards were lit; the interior of the box being otherwise dark. The eye movements of the subjects were recorded on a pen recorder. Seven black and white $2\frac{1}{2}$ inch square photographs were used as stimuli. Distribution of black and white was matched between pictures. They showed: (1) a group of penguins; (2) a bottle; (3) a house; (4) trees; (5) people sitting down; (6) a cup and saucer, and (7) people marching. Each child saw one of these pictures over six trials, together with each of the other pictures in turn. The picture selected for constant presentation and the left–right positioning of stimuli was varied between subjects according to a balanced design. Thus a subject would see penguins presented together on successive trials with a bottle, a house, trees, people sitting down, a cup and saucer and people marching. The next subject would then see the picture of a bottle presented constantly, and paired in turn with each of the other pictures. Total inspection time was 10 seconds for any one pair of pictures.

An analysis of variance of the results showed no significant difference between groups, but a highly significant difference between pictures. The relatively new picture of a pair was looked at for increasingly longer periods in preference to the relatively familiar one with each successive presentation. The interaction between groups and occasions did not reach significance. Nevertheless, inspection of the scores indicate that the effect of novelty was less marked for the autistic and subnormal children than it was for the normals. Table 16 demonstrates this. (A minus score signifies longer fixation time of the familiar and a plus sign longer inspection of the novel picture.)

The fact that subnormal and autistic children show similar tendencies in their inspection of relatively novel as compared with relatively familiar stimuli illustrates the possible fallacies in attempts to relate such behavioural data directly to the neurophysiological concepts of arousal. On physiological measures, such as EEG and PGR response, subnormals have on the whole been found to be under-aroused (Berkson, 1961), while over-arousal is claimed by Hutt et al. (1964, 1965a) for autistic children. Accepting their data, one would have to account for the relative lack of interest shown in novel stimuli as a function of under-arousal in the case of the subnormals and over-arousal in the case of the autistic children.

A more direct test of the arousal hypothesis put forward by Hutt et al. (1965a) was made by us in an EEG study (Hermelin and O'Connor, 1968). This experiment compared the amount of alpha waves in the EEG records of normal, subnormal and autistic children under conditions of darkness, as well as with continuous and also intermittent light and sound signals.

Although it is not universally accepted that a greater amount of alpha rhythm in the EEG means that one subject is less aroused than another, the presence or absence of a synchronized 8–13 c.p.s. rhythm, recorded from the occipital region of the head, has often been regarded as an indication of the state of alertness of the organism. In a waking subject, an increase in arousal is indicated by a change in the EEG pattern towards less regularity and higher frequency. However, when the subject is drowsy or somnolent, slower EEG waves can be replaced by the alpha rhythm if the subject's attention or interest is aroused. We therefore asked ourselves the following questions: (1) Did normal, subnormal and autistic children differ in their state of cortical arousal under resting

TABLE 16. DIFFERENCE SCORES BETWEEN INSPECTION TIMES FOR FAMILIAR AND NOVEL PICTURES BY GROUPS AND PICTURES
(means and standard deviations)

	Successive comparisons						
	1	2	3	4	5	6	7
Normal	-0.34 ± 3.68	-0.02 ± 3.54	1.35 ± 4.24	1.66 ± 4.36	0.91 ± 3.47	1.32 ± 4.21	2.39 ± 3.98
Severely subnormal	-1.80 ± 3.86	-0.02 ± 4.72	1.00 ± 4.68	-0.02 ± 4.28	-0.82 ± 4.81	2.90 ± 3.88	0.48 ± 5.03
Autistic	0.91 ± 3.18	-0.42 ± 3.83	-0.02 ± 3.37	-0.44 ± 2.71	-0.14 ± 3.01	1.40 ± 3.55	0.64 ± 3.71

conditions, i.e. while sitting quietly in a dark room? (2) Was the cortical arousal response to sound or light as measured by alpha blocking, different between the groups? (3) What were the differences between responses to continuous and short duration stimuli? (4) Were there any differences in adaptation rates?

Ten autistic, ten subnormal mongol and ten normal children took part in the experiment. Detailed information about them is given in Table 17.

Only those children whose records showed a minimum of 35 per cent of alpha waves of a frequency between 8 and 13 c.p.s. over a period of 2 minutes in resting conditions were accepted as subjects. In order to obtain ten such subjects for each group, seventeen autistic, sixteen subnormal and twelve normal children had to be tested. Thus, seven autistic, six mongol and two normal children had to be rejected as not fulfilling the criterion of a minimum of 35 per cent alpha waves in the EEG, while sitting in a dark room. The characteristics of the subjects whose records were excluded are also given in Table 17.

As can be seen by comparing accepted and rejected subjects, those with more alpha in the records tended to have higher chronological as well as mental ages. As the appearance of a stable rhythm in children is a function of age, this is perhaps not surprising. The only other difference between those autistic children with less and those with more alpha is in handedness. There were more right-handed children in the accepted than in the rejected group. As all recordings were made from the right side of the head, which in people with a left dominant hemisphere tends to show somewhat more alpha waves than the left one, this factor may possibly be relevant for the difference amounts of alpha found. The absence of any gross behavioural different between those children who were accepted and those rejected from the experimental groups, does not exclude the possibility that the final sample may have been atypical. It is possible that those autistic children who were excluded because of a low percentage alpha index might have responded differently from those with more alpha in their resting records. However, this qualification would also of necessity be true of the mongols.

The recordings were made by single channel telemetry. The apparatus has been described in some detail elsewhere (Hermelin and O'Connor, 1968). Briefly, the transmitter, consisting of a directly coupled amplifier, using three silicon planor transistors, and measuring $1\frac{3}{4}$ inches by 1 inch,

TABLE 17. CHARACTERISTICS OF AUTISTIC CHILDREN
(Subjects with less than 35 per cent alpha (N = 7))

	CA		MA				Reported onset	Handedness
			Verbal		Visual–motor			
	Years	Months	Years	Months	Years	Months		
Mean	8	8	3	3	4	11	Before 2 years N = 7	Right-handed N = 2
Range	5 15	0 0	1 4	11 8	4 6	0 3	After 2 years N = 0	Ambidextrous or left-handed N = 5

(Subjects with more than 35 per cent alpha (N = 10))

	CA		MA				Reported onset	Handedness
			Verbal		Visual–motor			
	Years	Months	Years	Months	Years	Months		
Mean	9	8	4	4	6	5	Before 2 years N = 8	Right-handed N = 7
Range	5 15	0 0	1 10	9 5	4 10	0 2	After 2 years N = 2	Ambidextrous or left-handed N = 3

was clipped onto the collar of the child's clothing. Two unipolar electrodes were placed over the right occipital region of the head. The child sat on a comforable chair in a darkened room, with an adult next to him. The sequence of stimulus condition is given in Table 18.

TABLE 18. SEQUENCE OF STIMULUS CONDITIONS
(DURATION 14 MINUTES)

(1) Two minutes' darkness
(2) Two minutes' intermittent light or sound (12 stimuli)
(3) Two minutes' continuous light or sound
(4) Two minutes' darkness
(5) Two minutes' intermittent sound or light (12 stimuli)
(6) Two minutes' continuous sound or light
(7) Two minutes' darkness

The stimuli were emitted from a loudspeaker, and a light placed in front of the subject at a distance of 4 feet and a height of 6 feet. The area of the light was a circle of 32 square inches and the sound signals had a frequency of 800 c.p.s. and an intensity of 75 db. The light intensity was matched to this (Stevens and Galanter, 1957).

The session began by the child sitting in the dark room for 2 minutes. This was followed by 2 minutes' intermittent and then by 2 minutes' continuous light or sound stimulation. After a further 2 minutes of darkness, those children who had been given visual stimulation first were now presented with auditory stimuli. Alternatively, those who had first been presented with sounds now were given visual stimulation. A final period of 2 minutes in darkness followed. The children were not required to shut their eyes, and apart from blinking kept them open throughout. The ten intermittent sound and light signals had a duration of 500 m. sec. and were presented at approximately 10 second intervals. We attempted to present each stimulus so that its onset coincided with a burst of alpha waves. Alpha rhythm was regarded as present when the record showed a train of waves of a frequency between 8 and 13 c.p.s. for at least $\frac{1}{2}$ second duration. In any one train of waves, the minimum accepted amplitude was half that of the largest wave in the train.

Mean alpha frequency was 9.4 c.p.s. in the normals, and 10.1 for the autistic as well as for the mongol children. However, alpha frequency in the groups was not statistically different. In order to be accepted for the experiment, a subject had to have a minimum of 35 per cent alpha waves in his resting record. This, as already stated, resulted in the rejection of seven autistic, six mongol and two normal records. In the case of the mongols, these rejected records showed a predominance of slow 4–7 c.p.s. activity. One of them, in addition, showed some low voltage fast activity of 14 c.p.s. The predominant rhythm in the records of six rejected autistic children was also at 4–7 c.p.s., with three records also showing bursts of low voltage fast activity. One autistic child had a predominance of such fast rhythms. A pattern of slow waves alternating with fast activity, with little or no alpha was also found in the two normal records. There was thus no clear difference according to diagnosis, in the characteristics of the EEG records of those subjects who did not meet the experimental criterion. There was also no observable behavioural difference between those children with more and those with less alpha rhythm in their records. Those who were excluded from the experiment seemed neither more nor less restless or aroused than those who were accepted. Some children who moved about a good deal during the experimental session, got up or even talked or cried, showed a great deal of alpha, while others who sat quietly showed very little. Thus the relationship between arousal as measured by the EEG and observable behavioural arousal was far from perfect. For the subjects accepted for the experiment, the mean percentage of alpha waves in the records in the last 30 seconds of the initial dark period was 53 per cent for the normal children, ranging from 35 to 83 per cent. For the mongols the corresponding figures were mean 53 per cent, range from 39 to 83 per cent, and for the autistic children mean 46 per cent, range 38–78 per cent. There was no significant difference between these percentage alpha scores.

The scores for the amount of alpha waves in all conditions is given in Table 19.

In scoring the records for the amount of alpha waves present in resting conditions, we compared three different, randomly selected 5-second periods within the first half minute in each of the three periods of darkness. This comparison resulted in a significant groups-by-periods interaction, which was due to the fact that in the first two dark periods the mongols had more alpha in their records, i.e. were less aroused, than the

TABLE 19. MEAN SCORES FOR AMOUNT OF ALPHA (IN SECONDS) FOR ALL
CONDITIONS (Optimal score 15 seconds)

	Normal	Autistic	Mongol
DARKNESS I			
Initial score	7.2	7.0	10.2
Adapted score	8.7	7.5	9.1
LIGHT SIGNAL			
Initial score	3.3	3.1	4.5
Adapted score	3.7	5.9	4.5
CONTINUOUS LIGHT			
Initial score	2.7	2.8	1.6
Adapted score	3.9	4.0	3.2
DARKNESS II			
Initial score	7.6	5.8	8.7
Adapted score	9.3	7.1	9.3
SOUND SIGNALS			
Initial score	5.7	5.2	7.5
Adapted score	7.0	4.8	7.1
CONTINUOUS SOUND			
Initial score	8.3	5.3	8.9
Adapted score	8.5	6.5	9.4
DARKNESS III			
Initial score	8.4	6.6	6.7
Adapted score	8.1	7.7	8.0

other two groups. During the last dark period, at the end of the experimental session, this difference was no longer present.

Another comparison was concerned with the amount of adaptation
within each period of darkness. Alpha at the beginning of each such period
was compared with alpha towards the end. There was a significant
adaptation effect, i.e. an increase in alpha waves within each 2 minutes of
darkness for all groups. No group differences were found.

Thus the EEG records under resting conditions gave no indication that the arousal level in the autistic children was different from that of the normals. The relatively low arousal level of the mongols at the beginning of the experiment confirms previous findings (Berkson et al., 1961).

The next stage of analysis was concerned with the reaction to stimuli. We found no difference for any of the groups between the amount of alpha blocking with intermittent as compared with continuous light stimulation. When the amount of alpha blocking in response to the first intermittent light signals was compared with that in response to later signals, we found a significant groups-by-conditions interaction. This was due to the fact that the autistic children showed a larger decrease in blocking response than the other two groups. This relative lack of sustained arousal to intermittent visual stimulation is in line with the results of behavioural measures, which show briefer visual inspection times for autistic children (O'Connor and Hermelin, 1967a). Thus, if such observations can be related to arousal in any way, they do not seem to indicate a visual avoidance due to high arousal levels, but rather to a fast decrease in an arousal or orientation response. No such differences in adaptation were found with continuous visual stimulation.

The responses to sound differ from those to light in several ways. In contrast to visual stimulation, intermittent sound resulted in significantly more alpha blocking than continuous sound. Also, in contrast to the conditions where light was used, neither intermittent nor continuous sound resulted in an adaptation effect in any of the groups. Responses, as measured by alpha blocking were as marked at the end of a 2-minute period of auditory stimulation as they were at the beginning.

Comparing the various conditions with each other, we found that all subjects had significantly less alpha waves in the records when in stimulated than when in resting conditions. As one would expect, all showed significantly more alpha blocking under visual than under auditory stimulation. This difference was of the same magnitude for all groups when the effect of intermittent lights and sounds were compared. However, in comparing the difference on alpha blocking under conditions of continuous visual with those under continuous auditory stimulation, the difference was significantly greater for the normals and mongols than it was for the autistic children. Thus the autistic children were relatively more aroused by a continuous sound than the other subjects.

Summarizing these EEG results, they show that fewer autistic than normal children have a predominance of 8–13 c.p.s. waves in their resting records. The same is true of mongol children, and the records of the subjects with little or no alpha are not dissimilar. They tend to show a predominance of slow 4–7 waves, and in some records occasional bursts of fast low voltage activity were also present. In those records with sufficient alpha, the mean alpha frequency as well as the mean percentage alpha is statistically the same for all three groups. The resting records of the autistic children show the same amount of adaptation as those of the normals, while the mongols show less evidence of arousal in the first two resting periods.

All children show a similar amount of alpha blocking in response to intermittent and continuous light stimulation. However, the autistic children adapt significantly more to intermittent lights, and probably orientated less and less towards them. In contrast, the autistic children tend to be more aroused by sound than the other subjects, at least when it is continuous.

Somewhat simplifying the results, the autistic children do not differ from normals in their cortical arousal state as measured by alpha blocking, in resting conditions. They orient as much as the others towards light, but adapt more quickly to it, i.e. the arousal is less sustained. Under conditions of sound stimulation on the other hand, they tend to have a relatively higher arousal level than do the other groups. The results are complicated by the fact that in the case of light these differentiating effects are only present in intermittent and in the case of sound in continuous stimulation conditions.

These results show that to talk of a general level of either high or low arousal in autistic children is too simplified a view. Firstly, there is the relevance of the particular measure used, and arousal as measured by these particular EEG indices may or may not correlate with, for instance, autonomic measures. Nor need the latter correlate with each other. Secondly, the correspondence between physiological and behavioural arousal is by no means simple. While Lanzing et al. (1959) and Fedio et al. (1961) for instance, found such a correspondence with normals, Hermelin and Venables (1964) failed to find a similar relationship with subnormals. Finally, even if only one measure is used, the relative position of groups on the arousal continuum may vary between resting and stimulated conditions, between intermittent and continuous stimulation, between orienting and adaptation responses, and between responsiveness to stimuli in different modalities. The present experiment has only begun to investigate some of these variables.

RESPONSES TO PEOPLE

So far we were concerned with measures of responsiveness to various relatively simple stimuli and stimulus dimensions. Social responsiveness on the other hand consists of multidimensional responses to complex multidimensional stimulation. Nevertheless, we think it fruitful to consider the social responses of autistic children in this context.

One of the most universally agreed symptoms of childhood autism is the absence of meaningful social and emotional relationships. The very name of the syndrome is meant to illustrate this characteristic of "aloneness" which Kanner observed. Since then, nearly all observers of autistic children have remarked on this phenomenon, though the underlying reasons and mechanisms for it have been variously interpreted. The impairment of emotional relationships is a *sine qua non* in the diagnostic points of Creak *et al.* (1961). Hutt *et al.* found it in their experimental studies, and Rutter (1966) finds that it is often present after other symptoms have subsided. Most investigators agree that social and emotional withdrawal is more typical of the younger than the older child, and more marked in relation to other children than to adults. Complex interactions between people are by their very nature difficult to investigate in the laboratory under controlled conditions. Heisenberg's finding that observation itself may change the observed phenomena, probably applies as much to social situations as to many physical ones. Therefore experimental studies may perhaps seem to have a limited validity as compared with sensitive and perceptive observations made by clinicians. Nevertheless, studies such as Argyle's (1967) have recently made a fresh attempt to form a closer link between the main body of experimental psychology and the study of interpersonal relationships. For this, social contacts are treated as situations in which social skills are utilized. Methods akin to those which have been developed for analysis of sensory–motor abilities in laboratory experiments are used to analyse interpersonal contacts. Even more basic are questions dealing with orienting responses and attention in situations involving other people. While lack of social skill may simply result in an indifference with regard to social interaction a deliberate withdrawal could presumably result in diminished orienting and approach responses. In our studies of the social responses of autistic children, we were concerned to observe their behaviour in the context of similar response variables to other, non-social stimuli. We do not question the observation that autistic children interact less with other people than children who are not autistic. What we consider necessary to establish is whether their total pattern of reactions and the relative magnitude and deviation of their responses to people as compared with responses to other stimuli is indeed so strikingly different from that of other children.

Walters and Parke (1964) have proposed an analysis of social behaviour in terms of orienting and attending responses. They suggest that the role of distance receptors is of primary importance in the development of social responsiveness in infancy and early childhood. Studies with normal infants support the conclusion that the origins of social attachment can not be regarded either as the result of generalization from need reduction alone (Schaffer and Emerson, 1964a) nor as depending primarily on physical contact between mother and baby (Schaffer and Emerson, 1964b).

Fantz (1961), presenting 1- to 6-month-old infants with a face, facial features in a scrambled pattern, and also a facial outline without features, found that most infants exhibited a preference for the face. Kagan and Lewis (1964) in addition to deviation of visual fixation, also used cardiac acceleration as an index of attention. With 6-month-old infants they found that photographs of male and female faces elicited more sustained attention than other visual stimuli, and moreover, female faces elicited more response than male faces. They also found responses to the human voice, male and female, greater than those to other auditory stimuli. Thus, already during the first 6 months of life, visual and auditory social stimulation seems to elicit specific responsiveness.

Smiling has frequently been used as an index of social responsiveness, and the human face has been reported as the most effective visual stimulus for eliciting smiling. Few infants, however, smile during and after feeding, and most smiles occur in response to the sight of the human face, and before physical contact with the infant occurs (Dennis, 1935). More recent observations suggest that auditory–vocal stimulation is even more effective in evoking early smiling responses (third week) than is a visual stimulus (Wolff, 1963). On the other hand, proprioceptive–tactual stimulation alone failed to evoke smiling until between the fourth and sixth weeks. Brackhill (1958) has demonstrated that the smiling response may be strengthened or weakened according to well-established learning principles. There would appear to be no studies concerned with early smiling responses in autistic children. Nevertheless, it is interesting that in normal infants this social response is elicited, maintained and modified through the presentation of visual and auditory stimuli. We have previously demonstrated that the distance receptors in autistic children do not play the dominant part in sensory organization as they do in normals, and there are many observations stressing the importance of proximal receptors in the exploration of the environment in autistic children. The importance of the distance receptors in the development of social responses are confirmed by findings of Scott (1964) that congenitally blind children tend to be socially retarded. Admittedly, there are difficulties regarding neurophysiological involvement in such children; nevertheless, the findings are suggestive.

The relative lack of response to speech, and the resulting impairment in communication may also contribute very largely to the impression of social unresponsiveness in autistic children. We found (O'Connor and Hermelin, 1965b) than non-mongol subnormal children responded to a light more frequently than to a sound, even when the light was less intense than the simultaneously presented sound. However, when the words "come here" were presented together with the light, the response to these words, as compared with those to the sounds, increased significantly in these subnormal children. No such significant increases occurred in the mongol and autistic children. This contrasts sharply with Wolff's (1963) findings that even in the very young babies a voice evokes more response than other sounds. However, such results alone could not account for the unresponsiveness of autistic children to some kinds of social stimulation. The mongols about whom no observations in regard to social withdrawal have ever been made, show the same relative unresponsiveness to the human voice in this experiment.

A hypothesis linking social unresponsiveness with a failure to process some incoming sensory information adequately, seems in better accordance with the facts than one regarding this symptom as a consequence of disturbed mother–child relations. This is particularly relevant in the light of the accumulating evidence that infants below the age of 6 months do not develop specific attachments (Walters and Parke, 1965). Infantile autism, however, is in a great many cases supposed to be present from birth and the lack of reactivity to many sensory stimuli does seem to be observable from birth onwards. An absence of attachment to people could be regarded as only one instance of a general inability to process stimuli adequately.

That there are some dimensions of response to people, along which autistic children do not behave differently from controls of matched age and intelligence, have been demonstrated in two experiments already mentioned (Hermelin and O'Connor, 1963; O'Connor and Hermelin, 1963b). The first of these measured the number of orienting responses towards various stimuli. In one of these conditions the child and an adult were in an otherwise empty room for a period of 9 minutes. For the first 3 minutes of this period the adult sat still and silent, behaving as passively as possible. During three subsequent minutes, attempts at physical contact were made, either cuddling or tickling the child and engaging him in play. In the third 3-minute period the child was asked questions and required to carry out simple verbal commands. The child's behaviour was observed and recorded throughout. An analysis of the results showed that there was no significant difference between the groups in the number of approaches or responses they made, as long as these contacts were non-verbal. However, speaking or responding to speech did differentiate the groups, and many autistic children gave no indication that they understood what the experimenter was saying, or that they paid any attention to her when she spoke. As has already been mentioned, all children did orientate significantly more often and for longer periods towards the person in the room than towards pictures, music and toys. The subsequent experiment confirmed this last finding (O'Connor and Hermelin, 1963b). In this the physical distance of the subject from various stimulus objects at the end of a room was measured and compared. These objects were a box, a rocking platform, a blanket, a life-size, three-dimensional model of a woman, a person and a voice talking to the child through a loud-speaker. It was found that subnormal children spent significantly more time in the vicinity of the box, blanket and rocking platform than the autistic group, but that there were no differences for the remaining stimulus conditions. The children spent significantly more time near the person than near any of the other stimuli. For the autistic group, this was the only condition in which the score was significantly different from the five others. The subnormal children, in addition to spending significantly more time near the person than near any other stimulus, also spent less time near the model and the loudspeaker than they did near the platform and box.

Many clinicians would maintain that many autistic children, even while coming up to an adult, show less facial expression and use fewer expressive gestures than do controls groups. However, the relative absence of such behavioural features does not necessarily imply a selective social unresponsiveness. The results of the ITPA showed that the lowest performance on any subtest was achieved by the autistic children on the test in which they were required to demonstrate the use of objects by gestures. On the other hand, the subnormal children performed at normal level on this item. Thus the absence of expressive gestures is not confined to the social situation, but must be regarded as a more general disability in performing a specific skill. It may be useful to measure more limited and specific variables relevant to social interaction. One reported characteristic of autistic children, for example, is their supposed tendency to avoid looking at other people directly, and to avert their own gaze when being looked at.

Two final studies in this series used visual fixation time as a measure of response. The experiments have already been described in a previous chapter (O'Connor and Hermelin, 1967a). In the first, the subject viewed two lighted display cards in an otherwise dark box, and the direction and duration of his eye fixation was recorded. In this study, seven pairs of cards were presented, one pair being a photograph of a face and the same facial features in a scrambled pattern. We used three groups; normal, subnormal and autistic children. The autistic and subnormal children were of the same mental and chronological age, and the chronological age of the normals was matched to the mental ages of the other groups. Though the autistic children had lower fixation scores than the other two groups for all the display cards, they looked longer at the pair of cards showing scrambled and unscrambled faces than on any other stimulus pair. The two other groups also had the highest fixation scores for this pair of cards. Comparing the members of a pair with each other, all groups looked significantly more at the unscrambled than at the scrambled face. The autistic children did indeed look less often at the photograph of a human face than did the other children, but they also looked less at everything else. However, if their own fixation time is taken at a base line, they show more interest in the picture of a human face than they show in other pictures.

Our last study was concerned with gaze avoidance (O'Connor and Hermelin, 1967a). This has frequently been reported in autistic children, who are supposed to avert their eyes when others look at them. We reasoned that if this was a valid observation, then autistic children might be expected to look more readily at a human face with its eyes closed than one with its eyes open and directly looking at them. To carry out such an experiment, we cut away the corners of the display box previously used and put curtains in front of the resulting openings. The experimenter could put his head through these curtains into the box, and the time the child spent looking at his face could be recorded as previously. The experimenter put his head equally often in the right or left side opening of the box, and half the time he looked at the child, while on the other occasions his eyes were closed. There was no difference for any of the groups in the amount of time spent looking at the face with eyes open or closed, and the face was significantly longer fixated than any of the pictures which had been presented previously.

We have thus specified two dimensions of social contact, physical distance and visual fixation, along which autistic children do not differ from normal and subnormal controls. Though our results are limited, we would nevertheless suggest that it might be fruitful to look at the social and interpersonal behaviour of autistic children in terms of the absence of simple skills which are basic to the more complex skills involved in social and linguistic behaviour.

SUMMARY

Responsiveness to stimulation depends on the nature of the stimuli including features such as their modality, intensity and degree of novelty, and on the arousal level of the organism. States of arousal can be measured in terms of physiological indices, or in terms of behaviour. In the first instance, such measures include cortical and autonomic activity, in the latter case measures of attention or vigilance are often used. Such different measures are not always consistent with each other, indicating that there may be varying degrees of responsiveness co-existing in different systems, rather than one general arousal state.

Attempts to associate characteristics of behaviour of autistic children with over-arousal have been made. Some theories explain autistic behaviour as an attempt to control and reduce a chronically high state of arousal by limiting sensory input. Such an approach resembles Pavlov's concept of "protective inhibition".

One of our studies showed that autistic children have a greater amount of stimulus-independent behaviour than subnormal controls. These apparently random motor movements did not affect the level of responses to specific stimuli, which closely paralleled that of the controls. Though autistic children responded as often to stimulation as did the controls, their attention was sustained over a shorter period. Though visual inspection was brief, differential fixation time between simultaneously presented displays was similar to that of normal as well as subnormal children. There were tendencies to longer inspection times for novel as compared with familiar displays for all children, though these were most marked in the normal group. The hypothesis of preference for sameness as a defence against over-arousal receives no support from those results. It is also made less likely by the finding that severely subnormal children, who have been found to be under-aroused on some physiological indices had similar scores to the autistic group.

An EEG study compared the degree of alpha blocking in autistic, normal and mongol children. Telemetric records of the amount of alpha rhythm in darkness and during continuous and intermittent light and sound stimulation were obtained. A higher proportion of autistic and mongol children than of normals had to be excluded because of a low alpha index in resting conditions. In the case of the autistic children this may be associated with their relatively younger chronological and mental ages, or may be explained by the lack of clear laterality in the majority of this group. In connection with this last point, it is of interest that Oldfield has recently suggested that handedness is not a matter of speed or precision, but is concerned chiefly with the directness of connection and availability of expressive acts. Although basically similar in terms of responsiveness to the control groups, alpha blocking in autistic children adapted faster to intermittent light stimuli. This finding is consistent with the relatively shorter inspection times of visual displays. On the other hand, autistic children showed less alpha blocking, i.e. remained more responsive to continuous sound stimulation than did the other groups. This relatively high level of responsiveness is in contrast to observations that as far as behavioural responses are concerned, the children tend to ignore auditory stimuli.

Though attention to stimuli was overall less sustained in autistic children, they gave relatively more responses to a person than to other stimuli and looked longer at a picture showing a face than at other visual displays. They also looked as much at a human face with closed as with open eyes, giving no indication of "gaze avoidance". Our results gave no support to the view that the behaviour of autistic children towards people or images of people is specifically impaired in comparison with their behaviour towards objects.

CHAPTER 5

CONCLUSIONS

AUTISM AND MENTAL SUBNORMALITY

The association between autism and mental subnormality in children, if not complete, is certainly extensive. Lotter's (1967) figures quoted in the first chapter, make it unnecessary to argue the matter further. Either a common factor is associated both with autism and subnormality, or one is associated with the other. Whatever the origin of the disorder, the level of intelligence does not improve with age (Rutter, 1966b) and in many cases remains at the level of mild or severe subnormality. For this reason our controls were chosen from among children of subnormal intelligence or from younger normal children. Our assumption was that any differences which might then be found between the groups could be attributed to the special nature of the syndrome of childhood autism, and not to mental deficiency as such.

However, even given differences between subnormal and autistic children, these could still be due to either developmental or deviant characteristics of one of the groups. In other words, even where we did find differences, it is important to account for them in either quantitative (developmental) or qualitative (deviant) terms. Thus developmental factors might account for the difference found between subnormal and autistic children in making correct discrimination responses between two shapes, and between differently angled lines. Likewise the inability of the autistic children to imitate a serial order arrangement might be explained in terms of differentially retarded cognitive development.

When we consider the shorter visual inspection times, the apparently different hierarchial order of sensory input, and the relatively greater utilization of motor cues in the autistic than in the subnormal groups, a purely developmental hypothesis seems less likely. There is now considerable evidence refuting the suggestion that touch precedes vision in normal

121

development. This includes evidence of the earlier development of visual than of tactual discrimination, and the dominance of visual over tactual information in sensory conflict situations. Thus the relative inability of autistic children to make adequate use of visual cues may well be a deviant rather than a purely developmental phenomenon.

The relatively greater impairment in the appreciation of syntactical and meaningful verbal structures, and the similarity of the recall capacity for randomly and non-randomly ordered words by the autistic children, also seems a result which is qualitatively different from that of even very backward or very young children.

On the other hand, performance based on the use of motor rather than visual cues as well as verbal rote memory capacity are at a higher level than is indicated by the mental ages of the autistic children. However, even these findings apply more to those children with a lower level of cognitive development and to those who have not developed speech. Autistic children who function on a somewhat higher mental age level and have some language capacity, obtained results which in so far as they differ from those of the subnormal controls, do so in a developmental rather than in a deviant manner. Thus within the group of autistic children tested by us, not only levels of attainment, but also the strategies used to reach such levels differed in some experiments.

CLINICAL AND EXPERIMENTAL DESCRIPTIONS OF AUTISM

In attempting to analyse the performance of a group of autistic children, we obtained a set of results which can be used to describe a typical autistic child as seen from an experimental point of view. Alongside such a description can be set a clinical one. In spite of the uncertainties of diagnosis and the heterogeneity of the group of children called autistic, certain behavioural characteristics are now commonly regarded as typical. The two main symptoms described by Kanner as "aloneness" and "insistence on sameness" are still regarded as essential for a diagnosis of autism. In addition to this inability to form adequate social relationships and to tolerate change, the most widely agreed symptom is absence or abnormality of speech development. Stereotyped and manneristic behaviour is commonly found, and responses to sensory stimuli in various modalities, but particularly to sounds, is often regarded as being abnormal.

Cognitive retardation of varying severity and generality is present, and an inability to play, and a generally very restricted and repetitive behaviour repertoire is observed.

In addition to this delineation of the syndrome, which has been summarized most clearly by Rutter (1966a), some other supposedly outstanding characteristics of infantile autism have been mentioned. Of these, over-arousal (Hutt et al.), dissociation between memory and perception (Rimland) and impairment of the input mechanism (Anthony) have been of special interest.

The results of our investigations support some of the above observations, whereas we found little or no support for others. They also gave rise to the following additional or alternative conclusions:

(1) The picture of autistic children which emerges from our experimental results, does not include a marked and distinct aloofness from other people. The autistic children in our studies responded less frequently and for a shorter time to a whole range of stimuli, including, but not singling out, those of a quasi-social nature. In comparing different conditions rather than groups, we found the children more responsive to a person and the representation of a person than to other stimuli. We also found no evidence of gaze avoidance.

(2) The brief visual inspection time shown by the autistic children in our experiments was paralleled by a relatively fast adaptation to light at the cortical level. There thus seems to be fairly firm evidence that the children attend to visual stimulation for a briefer period than normal or subnormal controls.

(3) The autistic children tested by us were relatively unresponsive to verbal as well as non-verbal auditory stimuli, and the same was true of mongol children, though not of non-mongol subnormals. However, mongols and autistic children behaved differently in regard to cortical arousal in response to auditory stimulation. Only the autistic children showed a more extended effect of continuous sound in their EEG records. This illustrates the fact that though the autistic children do resemble subnormal controls in many respects, the underlying mechanisms giving rise to this behaviour may differ on occasion.

(4) In visual–motor discrimination tasks, the autistic children seemed to rely mainly on distinct motor response cues. When such cues were

provided they could often solve the task presented, whereas they could not do so in their absence. There seemed to be only a limited ability to process visual data, though the processing in this instance was more efficient than in the case of verbal sequences.

(5) The autistic children in our experiments had immediate auditory rote memories which were better than those of subnormals and as good as, or better than those of normal children of similar mental age. However, the recall capacity of the control groups improved significantly more when syntactical and meaningfully related material was presented, than did that of the autistic children. There was little difference in recall of sense or nonsense in the autistic groups. On the other hand, the autistic children showed stronger recency effects than the other groups. These effects were less marked when the material was presented in the form of pictures instead of verbally.

Thus on the basis of our results, autistic children show more activity which is non-stimulus directed than do subnormal children. Their orientation towards visual stimuli, including people, is less sustained and they are less able to use visual information in perceptual motor tasks.

While behavioural as well as physiological responses tend to be relatively brief in conditions of visual stimulation, the autistic children showed more cortical responsiveness than the control groups following an auditory stimulus. In contrast to this relatively high cortical arousal, they gave fewer behavioural orientation responses to sounds than the other groups.

The autistic children did not vary in the amount of responsiveness according to whether sounds or words were used as stimuli. While phonological stress on words had the same facilitating effect on recall as it had for other children, the difference between recall efficiency of words arranged into sentences and randomly arranged word sequences was far less marked in the autistic than in the normal and subnormal children.

On the credit side, the autistic group had good rote memory and made efficient use of kinesthetic and motor feedback cues.

EVALUATION OF HYPOTHESES

Of those hypotheses put forward by others, we attempted to test observations concerning social and emotional withdrawal, over-arousal, resistance to change, and preference for proximal receptor stimulation. Withdrawal, remoteness and gaze-avoidance as defined by the experimental variables used, were not shown by this group of autistic children as compared with controls, except in relation to verbal signals. A brief inspection time was found for autistic children in regard to all displays, whether measured in terms of approach behaviour or visual fixation time. However, comparisons showed that they responded to a three-dimensional model of a person, to a photograph of a face and to a real person or face for more prolonged periods than to other non-social stimuli.

We found little evidence to justify an explanatory theory of autism in terms of general cortical over-arousal. In fact, with regard to visual stimulation, the EEG records suggested under- rather than over-responsiveness. No difference in resting conditions between autistic children and controls was shown in the arousal index used. Only in response to sound was there some indication of over-arousal. Though the higher level of "self-generated" behaviour and the long periods of non-directed gazing are both non-stimulus directed and could therefore be interpreted in terms of stimulus avoidance due to a state of over-arousal, there seems to us little justification for doing so. Firstly, self-generated behaviour in our experiment did not increase with increasing complexity of the situation. This is inconsistent with an arousal hypothesis. Secondly, the undirected gaze scores decreased in response to the presentation of the photograph of a face as compared with a circle. The photograph of the face is presumably more arousing than that of a circle presented in the same experiment, and it should therefore have had the opposite effect, i.e. increasing such random undirected gazing. The same argument applies a fortiore when self-generated behaviour is measured in response to situations in which a picture or a person is presented. If such self-generated behaviour is a measure of over-arousal, this should have increased in the presence of a more arousing stimulus, i.e. a person. It did not. A possible explanation of the high level of self-generated behaviour could be given in terms of stereotyped responses to the complex patterns of sensory input which will be discussed.

We already mentioned that our results support the hypothesis of proximal receptor preference in autistic children. This may be due either to a partial input block for visual and auditory signals, or more likely to an impairment in processing ability in regard to visual and particularly auditory information.

Our experiment concerned with resistance to change used very narrowly defined variables, and no such resistance was found in the situation concerned. However, a tendency to persist in a once-given response rather than to select an alternative one was found in subsequent experiments using different situations. These experiments are described very briefly below and illustrate that concepts such as "resistance to change", cannot be treated as unitary, but must be clearly defined and tested for their relevance to different situations. Whereas our experiments were concerned with exploratory and orienting responses to changing input, those carried out in collaboration with Frith (1968) investigated task directed behaviour. In some of her experiments, output in response to random or minimal input was recorded, while other tasks demanded a reflection of the structure of the input material in the responses.

NEW FINDINGS

In addition to those results which were obtained by testing hypotheses which arose from clinical observations, there are some findings which arose pursuant to hypotheses generated by our experiments. The very short visual inspection time which characterized the autistic group, has already been mentioned. This, and the extensive use made of motor cue in preference to visual cues, may indicate an incapacity to classify and interpret visually presented information. A more direct indication of this interpretation was the inability of the autistic children to arrange a number of squares of different sizes in sequential order.

With regard to the auditory modality, where the relatively efficient rote memory of autistic children facilitates investigation, we found a similar impairment in the appreciation of the order of words. There was a marked impairment in the use of the meaningful and syntactic aspects of language, and little difference in the ability to recall "sense" as compared with "nonsense".

The failure of autistic children in the appreciation of order and of a meaningful structure in the input must be seen as one of our main conclusions. More recent work by Frith (1968) re-examines and extends our findings. Her experiments are concerned with the reflection of the structure of the input in the output of normal, subnormal and autistic children.

Beginning with analyses of temporal order, she selected binary sequences of verbal and visual stimuli, and showed that normal children reflected the dominant structure of the presented series (input). This was demonstrated by the extraction of characteristic features of the presented sequences, and their exaggeration in recall (output). If the input was random, normal children imposed a non-random structure on this input in reproducing it; the older children imposing more complex and the younger simpler structures. Autistic children imposed a pattern on random material in a similar manner, although their patterns tended to be simpler. However, even when the input was structured, the autistic child behaved as if it were random, once more imposing his own simple structure on the data. In other words, the autistic child differs from the normal in the simplicity of the patterns he imposes on random data, and this may be a developmental difference. More important from our point of view and additionally, he differs from the normal child in lacking the capacity for feature extraction of ordered or structured input. Structured sequences are treated in the same way as random ones, by imposing structures which are themselves non-random, but independent of input.

This set of interesting findings seems to us to confirm our view that autistic children are deficient in the capacity to appreciate order or pattern where this involves extracting the structure of a sequence of stimuli. Whether this incapacity relates to conditions which are logical or semantic, spatial or temporal and modality dependent or independent, is a matter for further research.

ORIENTATIONS

In the last section we have considered some theories and hypotheses about autistic children, and evaluated them in terms of our experimental findings. If one considers the results which we have presented and the differences between the experimental and control groups, these differences can be described as developmental or deviant, quantitative or qualitative, due to subnormal or abnormal mental processes. By developmental differences we mean behaviour which is characteristic of younger children than the group examined, and by deviant behaviour we mean behaviour which would not have occurred in the developmental history of younger normal children.

The aloofness and isolation of autistic children and their inability to form adequate emotional relationships with others, is a symptom most markedly stressed by clinicians. This is a clearly deviant phenomenon, untypical of even very young normal children. Rutter (1966) reports that in his follow-up study, those autistic children who did poorly, retained their extreme affective isolation into late adolescence. Those who did better, became less autistic and less isolated, though loss of autism was not associated with a rise in measured intelligence.

In our experiments social responsiveness was measured in very simple and narrowly defined situations, which did not necessitate the mastering of a number of complex social skills and interactions which are present in most real life situations. If considered within the context of the limited behavioural repertoire of the autistic children, their social response behaviour did not differ from that of normal or subnormal controls. One possibility is that social withdrawal in some autistic children decreases with advancing age or intellectual development.

Cognitive processes might be similarly affected. Autistic children with mental ages of 5 years and above often obtained similar results in our experiments to those of subnormal children of the same chronological age and normal children of the corresponding mental age. However, the cognitively more backward autistic children, though often reaching a similar overall level of performance to those of matched controls, seemed to use different strategies. In several experiments, for instance, in which the children were matched for memory span, very retarded autistic children used redundancy or meaning, less efficiently than the controls, and relied more on either rote memory or on an imposition of simple patterns on the material. In visual–motor tasks, the more retarded autistic children used motor cues more and visual ones less efficiently than a mentally more advanced group.

One could thus conclude that the autistic child who is also severely retarded shows deviant cognitive behaviour in addition to retardation. On the other hand, autistic children with less intellectual impairment use similar cognitive strategies to subnormal and young normal children. It thus seems possible that affectively deviant behaviour in autistic children is somewhat alleviated as the child grows older, irrespective of intellectual development. On the other hand, abnormal as distinct from subnormal cognitive characteristics become less marked with a higher level of intellectual development, irrespective of chronological age.

The lack of feature extraction, together with the tendency to impose the same simple, repetitive patterns on random as well as on structural input, may account for an apparent paradox in the behaviour of autistic children. On the one hand, the spontaneous activity of such children is often highly structured, stereotyped, rigid and repetitive. On the other hand, they often tend to respond to meaningful and structured input from their environment in an apparently inappropriate and unpredictable manner.

It has been assumed (Wing, 1966; Rutter, 1966) that the inability of the autistic child to order its environment meaningfully, may give rise to alternative attempts at patterning. These attempts could account for the stereotypies and obsessional attachments to certain objects or their arrangement, and for the insistence on the rigid ordering of events. According to this view, such behaviour manifestations would be secondary in nature. An alternative hypothesis to account for obsessional and manneristic symptoms, as well as for inappropriate responses to stimuli would be the assumption of one single central deficit. A strong tendency to impose stimulus independent, simple, rigid and repetitive patterns on random as well as on structured, meaningful input, would lead to an impaired and limited ability for appreciation and reflection of order, pattern structure and meaning in the environment. A tendency to impose stimulus-independent patterns on structured input would be particularly limiting for the extraction of features from structures governed by complex and flexible rules. The more complex and flexible these rules, as, for instance, those determining play, social interaction or language, the more limited and inappropriate the resulting behaviour would be. It seems from our results that an impairment of this nature is more marked in the younger and cognitively more backward autistic children than in the older and more intelligent. It also appears that the deficit is to some extent modality dependent, and affects the auditory–vocal channels more than visual and particularly motor activity. Despite these qualifications we regard the inability of autistic children to encode stimuli meaningfully as their basic cognitive deficit.

REFERENCES

ABBOT, C. (1882) The intelligence of batrachians, *Science*, **3**, 66–7.

AINSWORTH, M. (1962) The effects of maternal deprivation: a review of findings and controversy in the context of research strategy, in *Deprivation of Maternal Care: a reassessment of its effects*, W.H.O. Public Health Papers, **14**, 87–165.

ANTHONY, J. (1958a) An experimental approach to the psychopathology of childhood autism, *Brit. J. Med. Psychol.* **31**, 211–25.

ANTHONY, J. (1958b) An aetiological approach to the diagnosis of psychosis in childhood, *Rev. Psychiat. Infant*, **25**, 89–95.

ANTHONY, J. (1962) Low grade psychosis in childhood, *Proceedings of the London Conference for the Scientific Study of Mental Deficiency*, vol. 2, B. W. Richards (Ed.), May & Baker, London.

ARGYLE, M. (1967) *Interpersonal Relations*, Penguin, London.

BARNETT, A. B. and GOODWIN, R. S. (1965) Averaged evoked electroencephalographic responses to clicks in the human newborn, *EEG Clin. Neurophysiol.* **18**, 441–50.

BENDER, L. (1947) Childhood schizophrenia: a clinical study of 100 schizophrenic children, *Amer. J. Orthopsychiat.* **17**, 40–56.

BENDER, L. (1956) Schizophrenia in childhood: its recognition, description and treatment, *Amer. J. Orthopsychiat.* **26**, 499–506.

BENDER, L. (1961) Childhood schizophrenia and convulsive states, *Recent Advances in Biological Psychiatry*, vol. 3, J. Wortis (Ed.), Plenum Press, New York.

BENDER, L. (1963) The origin and evolution of the Gestalt Function, the body image and delusional thoughts in schizophrenia, *Recent Advances in Biological Psychiatry*, vol. 5, J. Wortis (Ed.), Plenum Press, New York.

BENNER, B. and CASHDAN, S. (1967) Sensory processing and the recognition of forms in nursery-school children, *Brit. J. Psychol.* **58**, 101–4.

BERES, D. (1955) Ego deviations and the concept of schizophrenia, *Psychoanalytic Study of the Child*, **6**, 164–235.

BERKO, J. (1958) The child's learning of English morphology, *Word*, **14**, 150–77.

BERKSON, G. (1961) Responsiveness of the mentally deficient, *Amer. J. Ment. Defic.* **66**, 277–86.

BERKSON, G. and DAVENPORT, R. K. (1962) Stereotyped movements of mental defectives: I. Initial Survey, *Am. J. Ment. Defic.* **66**, 849–52.

BERKSON, G., HERMELIN, B. and O'CONNOR, N. (1961) Physiological responses of normals and institutionalised mental defectives to repeated stimuli, *J. Ment. Defic. Res.* **5** (1), 30–9.

BERLYNE, D. E. (1951) Attention to change, Brit. J. Psychol. 42, 269–78.

BERLYNE, D. E. (1958) The influence of complexity and novelty in visual figures on orienting responses, J. Exper. Psychol. 55, 289–96.

BERLYNE, D. E. (1960) Conflict, Arousal and Curiosity, London, McGraw-Hill.

BERNHAUT, M., GELLHORN, E. and RASMUSSEN, A. T. (1953) Experimental contributions to the problem of consciousness, J. Neurophysiol. 16, 21–36.

BETTELHEIM, B. (1967) The Empty Fortress, Collier-Macmillan, London, for the Free Press, New York.

BINET, A. (1894) Psychologie des Grands Calculateurs, Hachette, Paris.

BIRCH, H. G., TURKEWITZ, G., MOREAU, T., LEVY, L. and CORNWELL, A. C. (1966) Effect of intensity of auditory stimulation on directional eye movements in the human neonate, Animal Behaviour, 14, 93–101.

BLANK, H. R. (1959) Psychiatric problems associated with congenital blindness due to retrolental fibroplasia, New Outlook for the Blind, 53, 237–44.

BOURNE, H. (1955) Protophrenia, Lancet, 2, 1156–63.

BOUSFIELD, W. H. (1953) The occurrence of clustering in the recall of randomly arranged associates, J. Gen. Psychol. 49, 229–40.

BOWER, J. G. R. (1965) Stimulus variables determining space perception in infants, Science, 149, 88–9.

BOWER, J. G. R. (1966) Slant perception and shape constancy in infants, Science, 151, 832–4.

BOWLBY, J. (1952) Maternal care and mental health, W.H.O. Monograph No. 2, Geneva.

BRACKHILL, Y. (1958) Extinction of the smiling response in infants as a function of reinforcement schedule, Child Development, 29, 115–24.

BRAINE, M. D. S. (1963) On learning the grammatical order of words, Psychol. Rev. 70, 323–48.

BRASK, B. H. (1967) The need for hospital beds for psychotic children. An analysis based on a prevalence investigation in the county of Arlus, Ugeskr. Laeg. 129, 1559–70.

BREGER, L. (1965) Comments on building social behaviour in autistic children by use of electric shock, J. Exper. Res. Pers. 1, 110–13.

BRENNEN, W. M., AMES, E. W. and MOORE, R. W. (1966) Age differences in infants' attention to patterns of different complexity, Science, 151, 354–6.

BROADBENT, D. E. (1958) Perception and Communication, Pergamon Press, London.

BROADBENT, D. E. (1967) Les modeles et la formalisation du comportement, Colloques internationaux du centre national de la recherche scientifique, Paris.

BRONSTEIN, A. I., ITINA, N. A., KAMENETSKAIA, A. G. and SYTOVA, V. A. (1958) The orientation reaction in new-born infants, The Orienting Reflex and Exploratory Behaviour, Veronin, L. G. et al. (Eds.), Academy of Pedagogical Science, Moscow.

BROWN, R. (1965) Language: the system and its acquisition, in Social Psychology, Macmillan, London.

BROWN, R. and FRASER, C. (1963) The acquisition of syntax, *Verbal Behaviour and Learning*, C. N. Cofer and B. S. Musgrave (Eds.), McGraw-Hill, New York.

BRUNER, J. S. (1957) *Contemporary Approaches to Cognition*, Harvard University Press, Cambridge, Mass.

BRYANT, P. E. (1965) The transfer of sorting concepts by moderately retarded children, *Amer. J. Ment. Defic.* **70**, 291–300.

BRYANT, P. E. (1967a) Verbalisation and immediate memory of complex stimuli in normal and severely subnormal children, *Brit. J. Soc. Clin. Psychol.* **6**, 212–19.

BRYANT, P. E. (1967b) Verbal labelling and the learning of a complex discrimination by normal and severely subnormal children, *Lang. Speech*, **10**, 36–45.

BÜHLER, C., HETZER, H. and MABEL, F. (1928) Die Affektwirksamkeit von Fremheitseindrucken in ersten Lebensjahr, in *Zeitschrift Psychol. Abt.* **1**, 30–49.

CANTOR, G. N. (1963) Responses of infants and children to complex and novel stimulation, in *Advances in Child Development and Behaviour*, vol. 1, L. P. Lipsitt and C. C. Spiker (Eds.), Academic Press, New York.

CHAPMAN, A. H. (1957) Early infantile autism in identical twins: report of a case, *A.M.A. Arch. Neurol. Psychiat.* **54**, 621–3.

CHOMSKY, N. (1957) *Syntactic Structures*, Gravenhage, Netherlands Mouton.

CHOMSKY, N. (1961) An elementary linguistic theory, in *Psycholinguistics*, S. Saporta (Ed.), New York, Holt, Rinehart & Winston.

CONRAD, R. (1964) Acoustic confusions in immediate memory, *Brit. J. Psychol.* **55**, 75–84.

CONRAD, R. and MARY LOU RUSH (1965) On the nature of short-term memory encoding by the deaf, *J. Speech Hearing Disorders* **30**, 336–43.

CRAIK, F. I. M. (1966) Short-term memory: echo box plus search process, London Conference of the British Psychological Society.

CREAK, M. (1961) Schizophrenic syndrome in childhood: progress report of a working party, April 1961, *Cerebral Palsy Bull.* **3**, 501–4.

CREAK, M. (1963) Childhood psychosis: a review of 100 cases, *Brit. J. Psychiat.* **109**, 84.

CREAK, M. and INI, S. (1960) Families of psychotic children, *J. Child Psychol. Psychiat.* **1**, 156–75.

DARROW, C. W., JOST, H., SOLOMON, A. P. and MERGENER, J. C. (1942) Autonomic indications of excitatory and honeostatic effects on the electroencaphalogram, *J. Psychol.* **14**, 115–30.

DARROW, C. W., PATHMAN, J. and KRONENBERG, G. (1946) Level of autonomic activity and the EEG, *J. Exp. Psychol.* **36**, 355–65.

DEESE, J. (1961) From the isolated verbal units to connected discourse, in *Verbal Learning and Verbal Behaviour*, C. N. Cofer (Ed.), McGraw-Hill, New York, pp. 11–14.

DENNIS, W. (1935) An experimental test of theories of social smiling in infants, *J. Soc. Psychol.* **6**, 214–32.

DENNIS, W. and NAJARIAN, P. (1957) Infant development under environmental handicap, *Psych. Monogr.* **71**, Whole No. 436.

DESPERT, J. L. (1955) Differential diagnosis between obsessive-compulsive neurosis and schizophrenia in children, *Psychopathic Child*, **30**, 240–53.

DUNCAN, J. (1942) *The Education of the Ordinary Child*, Nelson, London.

DUSTMAN, R. E. and BECK, E. C. (1966) Visually evoked potentials: amplitude change with age, *Science*, **151**, 1013–15.

DUTTON, G. (1964) The growth pattern of psychotic boys, *Brit. J. Psychiat.* **110**, 101–3.

EARL, C. J. C. (1934) The primitive catatonic psychosis of idiocy, *Brit. J. Med. Psychol.* **14**, 230–53.

EISENBERG, L. (1956) The autistic child in adolescence, *Amer. J. Psychiat.* **112**, 607–12.

EISENBERG, L. (1966) Psychotic disorders in childhood, in *Biological Basis of Pediatric Practice*, R. E. Cooke (Ed.), McGraw-Hill, New York.

EISENBERG, L. and KANNER, L. (1956) Early infantile autism 1943–1955, *Amer. J. Orthopsychiat.* **26**, 556–66.

ELLINGSON, R. J. (1957) "Arousal" and evoked responses in the EEGs of newborns, *Proc. 1st Int. Cong. Neurol. Sci.* **3**, 57–60.

ELLINGSON, R. J. (1960) Cortical electrical responses to visual stimulation in the human infant, *EEG Clin. Neurophysiol.* **12**, 663–77.

ELLINGSON, R. J. (1964) Studies of the electrical activity of the developing human brain, in *Progress in Brain Research*, vol. 9, W. A. Himwich and H. E. Himwich (Eds.), Elserier, Amsterdam.

ELLINGSON, R. J. (1966) Development of visual evoked responses in human infants recorded by a response averager, *EEG Clin. Neurophysiol.* **21**, 403–4.

EPSTEIN, W. (1961) The influence of syntactical structure on learning, *Amer. J. Psychol.* **74**, 80–5.

EPSTEIN, W. (1962) A further study of the influence of syntactical structures on learning, *Amer. J. Psychol.* **75**, 121–6.

EPSTEIN, W., MILLER, G. A. and ISARD, S. (1963) Some perceptual consequences of linguistic rules, *J. Verb. Learn Verb. Behav.* **2**, 217–28.

FANTZ, R. L. (1961) The origin of form perception, *Scient. Amer.* **204**, 66–72.

FANTZ, R. L. (1965) Pattern discrimination and selective attention as determinants of perceptual development from birth, *Perceptual Development of Children*, A. H. Kidd and J. L. Rivoire (Eds.), Int. Univ. Press, N.Y.

FEDIO, P. M., MIRSKY, A. F., SMITH, W. J. and PARRY, D. (1961) Reaction time and EEG activation in normal and schizophrenic subjects, *EEG Clin. Neurophysiol.*, Amsterdam, **13**, 923–6.

FEIGENBAUM, E. A. (1963) The simulation of verbal learning behaviour. In: *Computers and Thought*, E. A. Feigenbaum and J. Feldman (Eds.), McGraw-Hill, New York.

FERRIS, G. S., DAVIS, G. D., HACKETT, E. R. and DORSEN, M. M. (1966) Maturation of visually evoked responses in human infants, *EEG Clin. Neurophysiol.* **21**, 404.

FERSTER, C. B. (1961) Positive reinforcement and behavioural deficits of autistic children, *Child Devel.* **32**, 437–56.

FERSTER, C. B. and DE MYER, M. K. (1961) The development of performances in autistic children in an automatically controlled environment, *J. Chron. Dis.* **13**, 312–45.

FERSTER, C. B. and DE MYER, M. K. (1962) A method for the experimental analysis of the behaviour of autistic children, *Amer. J. Orthopsychiat.* **32,** 89–98.

FRITH, U. (1968) Pattern detection in normal and autistic children, Ph.D. thesis. University of London.

FRITH, U. (1969) Emphasis and meaning in recall in normal and autistic children, *Lang. Speech,* **12,** 29–38.

FROSTIG, M. (1961) A developmental test of visual perception for evaluation of normal and neurologically handicapped children, *Perceptual Motor Skills,* **12,** 383–94.

FRY, D. B. (1958) Experiments in the perception of stress, *Lang. Speech,* **1,** 126–52.

FURTH, H. G. (1964) Research with the deaf: Implications for language and cognition, *Psychol. Bull.* **62,** 145–64.

FURTH, H. G. (1966) *Thinking Without Language: psychological implications of deafness,* Free Press, New York.

GHENT, L. (1961) Form and its orientation: a child's eye view, *Amer. J. Psychol.* **74,** 177–90.

GIBSON, E. J., PICK, A., OSSER, H. and HAMMOND, M. (1962) The role of grapheme-phoneme correspondence in the perception of words, *Amer. J. Psychol.* **75,** 554–70.

GILLIES, S. M. (1965) Some abilities of psychotic children and subnormal controls, *J. Ment. Defic. Res.* **9,** 89–101.

GOLD, S. and VAUGHAN, G. F. (1964) Classification of childhood psychosis, *Lancet,* **2,** 1058–64.

GOLDFARB, W. (1956) Receptor preferences in schizophrenic children, *Arch. Neurol. Psychiat.* **76,** 643–53.

GOLDFARB, W. (1961) *Childhood Schizophrenia,* Harvard University Press, Cambridge, Mass.

GOLDFARB, W., BRAUNSTEIN, P. and LORGS, I. (1956) A study of speech patterns in a group of schizophrenic children, *Amer. J. Orthopsychiat.* **26,** 544–55.

GRAHAM, F. K., MATARAZZO, R. G. and CALDWELL, B. M. (1956) Behavioural differences between normal and traumatised infants, *Psychol. Monogr.* **70,** 427–8.

HADLEY, J. M. (1941) Some relationships between electrical signs of central and peripheral activity. II. During "mental work", *J. Exptl. Psychol.* **28,** 53–62.

HARLOW, H. F. (1958) The nature of love, *Amer. Psychol.* **13,** 673–85.

HARRIS, C. S. (1963) Adaptation to displaced vision, *Science,* **140,** 812–13.

HARRIS, C. S. (1965) Perceptual adaptation to inverted, reversed and displaced vision, *Psychol. Rev.* **72,** 419–44.

HEBB, D. O. (1949) *The Organisation of Behaviour,* Wiley, New York.

HEIN, A. and HELD, R. (1962) A neural model for labile sensorimotor co-ordinations, in *Biological Prototypes and Synthetic Systems,* E. E. Bernard and M. R. Kolne (Eds.), vol. 1, pp. 71–4, Plenum Press, New York.

HELD, R. (1961) Exposure history as a factor in maintaining stability of perception and co-ordination, *J. Nerv. Ment. Dis.* **132,** 26–32.

HELD, R. (1965) Plasticity in sensory-motor systems, *Scient. Amer.* **213,** 84–94.

HELD, R. and FREEDMAN, S. J. (1963) Plasticity in human sensorimotor control, *Science*, **142**, 455–62.

HELD, R. and HEIN, A. (1963) Movement produced stimulation in the development of visually guided behaviour, *J. Comp. Physiol. Psychol.* **56**, 872–6.

HERMELIN, B. and O'CONNOR, N. (1963) The response and self-generated behaviour of severely disturbed children and severely subnormal controls, *Brit. J. Soc. Clin. Psychol.* **2**, 37–43.

HERMELIN, B. and O'CONNOR, N. (1964) Effects of sensory input and sensory dominance on severely disturbed children and on subnormal controls, *Brit. J. Psychol.* **55**, 201–6.

HERMELIN, B. and O'CONNOR, N. (1965) Visual imperception in psychotic children, *Brit. J. Psychol.* **56**, 455–60.

HERMELIN, B. and O'CONNOR, N. (1967a) Perceptual and motor discrimination in psychotic and normal children, *J. Genet. Psychol.* **110**, 117–25.

HERMELIN, B. and O'CONNOR, N. (1967b) Remembering of words by psychotic and subnormal children, *Brit. J. Psychol.* **58**, 213–18.

HERMELIN, B. and O'CONNOR, N. (1968) Measures of the occipital alpha rhythm in normal, subnormal and autistic children, *Brit. J. Psychiat.* **114**, 603–10.

HERMELIN, B. and VENABLES, P. H. (1964) Reaction time and alpha blocking in normal and severely subnormal subjects, *J. Exptl. Psychol.* **67**, 365–72.

HERNANDEZ-PEON, R., GUZMAN-FLORES, C., ALVAREZ, M. and FERNANDEZ-GUARDIOLA, A. (1956) Photic potentials in the visual pathway during "attention" and photic "habituation", *Fed. Proc.* **15**, 91–2.

HERSHENSON, M. (1964) Visual discrimination in the human newborn, *J. Comp. Physiol. Psychol.* **58**, 270–6.

HOUSE, BETTY J. (1964) The effect of distinctive responses on discrimination reversals in retardates, *Amer. J. Ment. Defic.* **69**, 79–85.

HOWARD, I. P. and TEMPLETON, W. B. (1966) The behavioural consequences of rotations and displacements of the optical array, Chapter 15. In *Human Spatial Orientation*, I. P. Howard and W. B. Templeton, Wiley, London.

HULL, C. L. (1943) *Principles of Behaviour*, Appleton-Century-Crofts, New York.

HUNT, E. B. (1962) *Concept Learning: an information processing problem*, Wiley, New York.

HUTT, S. J., HUTT, C., LEE, D. and OUNSTED, C. (1964) Arousal and childhood autism, *Nature*, **204**, 908–9.

HUTT, S. J., HUTT, C., LEE, D. and OUNSTED, C. (1965) A behavioural and electroencephalographic study of autistic children, *J. Psychiat. Res.* **3**, 181–98.

HUTT, C. and OUNSTED, C. (1966) The biological significance of gaze aversion with particular reference to the syndrome of infantile autism, *Behav. Sci.* **11**, 346–56.

HUTT, S. J. and VAIZEY, M. J. (1966) Differential effects of group density on social behaviour, *Nature*, **209**, 1371–2.

INHELDER, B. and PIAGET, J. (1958) *The Growth of Logical Thinking from Childhood to Adolescence*, Basic Books, New York.

136 REFERENCES

INHELDER, B. and PIAGET, J. (1964) *The Early Growth of Logic in the Child: classification and seriation*, Routledge and Kegan Paul, London.

ITARD, J. M. G. (1801) *The Wild Boy of Aveyron*, trans. G. & M. Humphrey (1932), Appleton Century, New York.

JASPER, H. H. (1954) Functional properties of the thalamic reticular system, in *Brain Mechanisms and Consciousness*, J. F. Delafresnaye (Ed.), Blackwell, Oxford.

JENSEN, A. R. (1964) Individual differences in learning: interference factors (U.S. Dept. of Health Coop. Project No. 1867).

KAGAN, J. and LEWIS, M. (1964) Studies of attention in the human infant, Monograph of Fels Research Institute, Yellow Springs, Ohio.

KALLMAN, F. J. and ROTH, B. (1956) Genetic aspects of pre-adolescent schizophrenia, *Amer. J. Psychiat.* **112**, 599–606.

KANNER, L. (1943) Autistic disturbances of affective contact, *Nervous Child*, **2**, 217–50.

KANNER, L. (1946) Irrelevant and metaphorical language in early infantile autism, *Amer. J. Psychiat.* **103**, 242–5.

KANNER, L. (1950) Review of psychiatric progress 1949: child psychiatry, mental deficiency, *Amer. J. Psychiat.* **106**, 515–18.

KANNER, L. (1954) To what extent is early infantile autism determined by constitutional inadequacies? *Proc. Ass. Res. Nerv. Ment. Dis.*, 378–85.

KEELER, W. R. (1958) Autistic patterns and defective communication in blind children with retrolental fibroplasia, in *Psychopathology of Communication*, P. H. Hoch and S. Zubin (Eds.), Grune & Stratton, New York.

KENDLER, H. H., KENDLER, T. S. and CARRICK, M. (1966) The effect of verbal labels on inferential problem solution, *Child Devel.* **37**, 749–63.

KENDLER, T. S. and KENDLER, H. H. (1967) Experimental analysis of inferential behaviour in children, in *Advances in Child Development and Behaviour*, vol. 3, L. P. Lipsitt and C. C. Spiker (Eds.), Academic Press, New York.

KENNARD, M. A. (1949) Inheritance of electroencephalogram patterns in children with behaviour disorders, *Psychosom. Med.* **11**, 151–7.

KENNARD, M. A. (1953) The electroencephalogram in psychological disorders: a review, *Psychosom. Med.* **15**, 95–115.

KISTIAKORSKAIA, M. I. (1965) Stimuli evoking positive emotions in infants in the first month of life, *Sov. Psychol. Psychiat.* **3**, 39–48.

KNIGHT, E. H. (1963) Some considerations regarding the concept of autism, *Dis. Nerv. Sys.* **24**, 224–9.

KNOBLOCH, H. and PASAMANICK, B. (1962) Etiological factors in "early infantile autism" and "childhood schizophrenia", Unpublished paper; read at the 10th International Congress of Pediatrics, Lisbon.

KUPALOW, P. S. and GANTT, W. H. (1928) On the relation between the strength of a conditioned stimulus and the magnitude of a conditioned reflex, in *Trudy Fizial Laboratories Pavlov*, **2**, 3–12.

LANSING, R. W., SCHWARTZ, E. and LINDSLEY, D. B. (1959) Reaction time and EEG activation under alerted and non-alerted conditions, *J. Exptl. Psychol.* **58**, 1–7.

LASHLEY, K. S. (1951) The problem of serial order in behaviour, in *Cerebral Mechanisms in Behaviour*, L. A. Jeffeess (Ed.), Wiley, New York.

LENNEBERG, E. H. (1964) A biological perspective of language, in *New Directions in the Study of Language*, E. H. Lenneberg (Ed.), M.I.T. Press, Cambridge, Mass.

LENNEBERG, E. H. (1967) *Biological Foundations of Language*, Wiley, New York.

LEWIS, M. M. (1936) *Infant Speech*, Routledge, London.

LINDSLEY, D. B. (1958) The reticular formation in perceptual discrimination, in *Reticular Formation of the Brain*, H. H. Jasper *et al.* (Eds.), London.

LIPSITT, L. P. (1963) Learning in the first year of life, in *Advances in Child Development and Behaviour*, vol. 1, L. P. Lipsitt and C. S. Spiker (Eds.), Academic Press, New York, pp. 147–95.

LOTTER, V. (1966) Epidemiology of autistic conditions in young children. I: Prevalence, *Soc. Psychiat.* **1**, 124–37.

LOTTER, V. (1967) Epidemiology of autistic conditions in young children. II: Some characteristics of the parents and children, *Soc. Psychiat.* **1**, 163–73.

✻ LOVAAS, O. I. (1966) A programme for the establishment of speech in psychotic children, in *Early Childhood Autism*, J. Wing (Ed.), Pergamon Press, London.

LOVAAS, O. I., SCHAEFFER, B. and SIMMONS, J. Q. (1965) Building social behaviour in autistic children by use of electric shock, *J. Exptl. Res. Pers.* **1**, 99–109.

LÖWENFELD, B. (1927) Systematisches Studium der Reactionen der Säuglinge auf Klänge und Geräusche, *Z. Psychol. Abt.* **1**, 62–96.

LURIA, A. R. (1961) *The Role of Speech in the Regulation of Normal and Abnormal Behaviour*, J. Tizard (Ed.), Pergamon Press, London.

McCARTHY, J. and KIRK, S. A. (1961) *The Illinois Test of Psycholinguistic Abilities. Experimental Edition*, Urbana, Illinois, University Illinois.

MACCOBY, E. E. (1967) Selective auditory attention in children, in *Advances in Child Development and Behaviour*, L. P. Lipsett and C. C. Spiker (Eds.), Academic Press, New York.

MACKINTOSH, N. J. (1965) Selective attention in animal discrimination learning, *Psychol. Bull.* **64**, 124–50.

McNEILL, D. (1965) Development of the semantic system, Unpublished paper, Center for Cognitive Studies, Harvard University, Harvard.

MAHLER, M. S., FURER, M. and SETTLAGE, C. F. (1959) Severe emotional disturbance in childhood: psychosis, in *American Handbook of Psychiatry*, S. Arieti (Ed.), Basic Books, New York, pp. 816–39.

MARKS, L. and MILLER, G. (1964) The role of semantic and syntactic constraints in the memorisation of English sentences, *J. Verb. Learn Verb. Bhvr.* **3**, 1–5.

MAYER-GROSS, W., SLATER, E. and ROTH, M. (1955) *Clinical Psychiatry*, Cassell, London.

MEIN, R. (1961) A list of words used in conversation of severely subnormal patients, Cell Barnes and Harperbury Group Hospital Management Committee.

MEIN, R. and O'CONNOR, N. (1960) A study of the oral vocabularies of severely subnormal patients, *J. Ment. Defic. Res.* pp. 130–43.

METZ, J. R. (1965) Conditioning generalised imitation in autistic children, *J. Exptl. Child Psychol.* **2**, 389–99.

MILLER, G. A. (1964) Language and psychology, in *New Directions in the Study of Language*, E. H. Lenneberg (Ed.), M.I.T. Press, Cambridge, Mass.

MILLER, G. A. and CHOMSKY, N. (1963) Finitary models of language users, in *Handbook of Mathematical Psychology*, vol. 2, R. Luce, R. Bush and E. Galanter (Eds.), Wiley, New York.

MILLER, G. A. and ISARD, S. (1963) Some perceptual consequences of linguistic rules, *J. Verb. Learn. Verb. Behvr.* **2**, 217, 228.

NESNIDALOVA, R. and FIALA, V. (1961) Kotazce Kannerova casncho detskeho autismu (on the question of Kanner's early infantile autism), *Ceskoslov. Psychiat.* **57**, 76–84.

ONONDAGA COUNTY SURVEY (1955) A special census of suspected-referred mental retardation, in *Comm. Ment. Hlth. Res.*, New York State Dept. Ment. Hyg. Rep.

O'CONNOR, N. and HERMELIN, B. (1959) Discrimination and reversal learning in imbeciles, *J. Ab. Soc. Psychol.* **59**, 409–13.

O'CONNOR, N. and HERMELIN, B. (1963a) *Speech and Thought in Severe Subnormality*, Pergamon Press, London.

O'CONNOR, N. and HERMELIN, B. (1963b) Measures of distance and motility in psychotic children and severely subnormal controls, *Brit. J. Soc. Clin. Psychol.* **3**, 29–33.

O'CONNOR, N. and HERMELIN, B. (1965a) Visual analogies of verbal operations, *Language and Speech*, **8**, 197–207.

O'CONNOR, N. and HERMELIN, B. (1965b) Sensory dominance in autistic imbecile children and controls, *Archiv. Gen. Psychiat.* **12**, 99–103.

O'CONNOR, N. and HERMELIN, B. (1967a) The selective visual attention of psychotic children, *J. Child Psychol. Psychiat.* **8**, 167–79.

O'CONNOR, N. and HERMELIN, B. (1967b) Auditory and visual memory in autistic and normal children, *J. Ment. Def. Res.* **11**, 126–31.

OLDFIELD, R. C. (1966) Things, words and the brain. (The Sir Frederick Bartlett lectures, No. 1) *Quart. J. Exptl. Psychol.* **18**, 340–53.

OSGOOD, C. E. (1957a) A behaviouristic analysis, in *Contemporary Approaches to Cognition*, Harvard Univ. Press, Cambridge, Mass.

OSGOOD, C. E. (1957b) Motivational dynamics of language behavior, in *Nebraska Symposium on Motivation*, Univ. Nebraska Press, Lincoln, U.S.A.

OVER, R. and OVER, J. (1967) Kinaesthetic judgements of the direction of line by young children, *Quart. J. Expl. Psychol.* **19**, 337–41.

PAPOUSEK, H. (1967) Experimental appetitional behaviour in human newborns and infants, in *Early Behaviour, Comparative and Developmental Approaches*, H. W. Stevenson, E. Hess and L. Reingold (Eds.), Wiley, New York.

PASAMANICK, B. and KNOBLOCH, H. (1963) Early feeding and birth difficulties in childhood schizophrenia: an explanatory note, *J. Psychol.* **56**, 73–7.

PAVLOV, I. P. (1927) *Conditioned Reflexes*, Clarendon Press, Oxford.

PIAGET, J. (1952) *The Origins of Intelligence in Children*, 2nd edn., International University Press, New York.

PIAGET, J. (1954) *The Construction of Reality in the Child*, Basic Books, New York.

PIAGET, J. (1965) Langage et Pensée, *Rev. Pract.* **15**, 2253–4.

PICK, H. L. and HAY, J. C. (1966) Visual and proprioceptive adaptation to optical displacement in children, in *Perceptual Development: Its relation to theories of intelligence and cognition*, Bethesda, National Institute of Health, 174–87.

PICK, A. D., PICK, H. L. and THOMAS, M. L. (1966) The role of grapheme–morpheme correspondences in the perception of braille, *J. Verb. Learn. Verb. Behav.* **5**, 298–300.

PICK, H. L., PICK, A. D. and KLEIN, R. E. (1967) Perceptual integration in children, in *Advances in Child Development and Behaviour*, vol. 3, L. P. Lipsitt and C. C. Spiker (Eds.), Academic Press, New York.

PITFIELD, M. and OPPENHEIM, A. N. (1964) Child rearing attitudes of mothers of psychotic children, *J. Child Psychol. Psychiat.* **5**, 51–57.

POLLACK, M. (1958) Brain damage and mental retardation in childhood schizophrenia, *Amer. J. Psychiat.* **115**, 422–8.

POLLACK, M. (1960) Comparison of childhood, adolescent and adult schizophrenics, *Arch. Gen. Psychiat.* **2**, 652–60.

POLLACK, M. and GOLDFARB, W. (1957) The face-hand test in schizophrenic children, *Arch. Neurol. Psychiat.* **77**, 635–42.

POLLACK, M. and GORDON, E. (1959) The face–hand test in retarded and non-retarded emotionally disturbed children, *Amer. J. Ment. Def.* **64**, 758–60.

POLLACK, M. and KREIGER, H. (1958) Oculomotor and postural patterns in schizophrenic children, *Arch. Neurol. Psychiat.* **79**, 720–6.

POPELLA, E. (1955) Zum krankheitsbild des fruhkindlichen autismus (On the syndrome of early infantile autism), *Nervenarzt*, **26**, 268–71.

RENSHAW, S. (1930) The errors of localisation and the effect of practice on the localising movement in children and adults, *J. Genet. Psychol.* **38**, 223–38.

RENSHAW, S. and WHERRY, R. J. (1931) Studies of cutaneous localisation. The age of onset of ocular dominance, *J. Genet. Psychol.* **39**, 493–96.

RICKMAN, V. V. (1928) Concerning the strength of conditioned reflexes, *Trudy Fizial Lab. Pavlova*, **2**, 13–24.

RIESEN, A. H. and AARONS, L. (1959) Visual movement and intensity discrimination in cats after early deprivation of pattern vision, *J. Comp. Physiol. Psychol.* **52**, 142–9.

✳ RIMLAND, B. (1964) *Infantile Autism*, Appleton-Century-Crofts, New York.

ROCK, I. and HARRIS, C. S. (1967) Vision and touch, *Scientific American*, **5**, 96–107.

ROCK, I. and VICTOR, J. (1963) Vision and touch: an experimentally created conflict between the two senses, *Science*, **143**, 594–6.

ROSS, I. S. (1959) Presentation of a clinical case: an autistic child, in *Pediatric Conferences* **2**, 1–13.

RUDEL, R. and TEUBER, H. L. (1963) Discrimination of direction of line in children, *J. Child Psychol. Psychiat.* **56**, 892–8.

RUNDLE, A. T., DUTTON, G. and GIBSON, J. (1959) Endocrinological aspects of mental deficiency: I. Testicular function in mongolism, *J. Ment. Def. Res.* **3**, 108–15.

RUNDLE, A. T. and SYLVESTER, P. E. (1962) Endocrinological aspects of mental deficiency: II. Maturational status of adult males, *J. Ment. Def. Res.* **6**, 87–93.

RUNDLE, A. T. and SYLVESTER, P. E. (1963) Endocrinological aspects of mental deficiency: III. Growth and development of young males, *J. Ment. Def. Res.* **7**, 10–21.

✕RUTTER, M. (1966a) Behavioural and cognitive characteristics, in *Early Childhood Autism: Clinical, Educational and Social Aspects*, J. Wing (Ed.), Pergamon Press, Oxford.

RUTTER, M. (1966b) Prognosis: psychotic children in adolescence and early adult life, in *Childhood Autism: Clinical, Educational and Social Aspects*, J. Wing (Ed.), Pergamon Press, Oxford.

RUTTER, M. (1967) Psychotic disorders in early childhood, in *Recent Developments in Schizophrenia*, A. J. Coppen (Ed.), *Brit. J. Psychiat.*, Special publication I.

SCHACHTER, M. (1958) Contribution a l'etude de l'autisme infantile precoce de Kanner, *Pediatre*, **13**, 175–91.

SCHAIN, R. J. and YANNET, H. (1960) Infantile autism: An analysis of 50 cases and a consideration of certain neurophysiologic concepts, *J. Pediat.* **57**, 560–7.

SCHEERER, M., ROTHMANN, E. and GOLDSTEIN, K. (1945) A case of *Idiot Savant:* an experimental study of personality organisation, *Psychol. Monogr.* **58**.

SCHOPLER, E. (1965) Early infantile autism and receptor processes, *Arch. Gen. Psychiat.* **13**, 327–35.

SCHOPLER, E. (1966) Visual versus tactile receptor preferences in normal and schizophrenic children, *J. Abn. Psychol.* **71**, 108–14.

SCHAFFER, H. R. and EMERSON, P. E. (1964a) The development of social attachments in infancy, *Monograph of Society for Research into Child Development*, **29**, 3.

SCHAFFER, H. R. and EMMERSON, P. E. (1964b) Patterns of response to physical contact in early human development, *J. Child Psychol. Psychiat.* **5**, 1–13.

SCOTT, R. R. (1964) The socialization of the blind child, Unpublished paper. Russell Sage Foundation, New York.

SHARPLESS, S. and JASPER, H. (1956) Habituation of the arousal reaction, *Brain* **79**, 655–80.

SHERRINGTON, C. S. (1960) *The Integrative Action of the Nervous System*, Cambridge University Press, London.

SIMON, G. B. and GILLIES, S. M. (1964) Some physical characteristics of a group of psychotic children, *Brit. J. Psychiat.* **110**, 104–7.

SKINNER, B. F. (1938) *The Behaviour of Organisms*, Appleton-Century-Crofts, New York.

SKINNER, B. F. (1957) *Verbal Behaviour*, Appleton-Century-Crofts, New York.

SMITH, K. V. and GREENE, P. (1963) A critical period in maturation of performance with space-displaced vision, *Percept. Mot. Skills*, **17**, 627–36.

SMITH, K. V. and WANGO, L. (1963) Sensory feedback analysis of specialization of movement in learning, *Percept. Mot. Skills*, **19**, 749–59.

SMITH, K. V., ZWERG, C. and SMITH, N. J. (1963) Sensory feedback analysis of infant control in the behavioural environment, *Percept. Mot. Skills*, **16**, 725–32.

SODDY, K. (1964) The autistic child, *The Practitioner*, **192**, 525–33.

SOKOLOV, Y. N. (1954) The orienting reflex and problems of reception, Report to the Conference on Problems of Psychology, in *Recent Soviet Psychology* (1961), N. O'Connor (Ed.), Pergamon Press, Oxford.

SOKOLOV, Y. N. (1958) *Perception and the Conditioned Reflex*, University of Moscow Press, Moscow.

SPENCE, K. W. (1945) An experimental test of the continuity and non-contiouity scores of discrimination learning, *J. Exptl. Psychol.* **35**, 253–66.

SPITZ, H. H. and HOATS, D. L. (1961) Experiments on perceptual curiosity behaviour in mental retardates, in Report NIMH, Grant M-4533.

SPITZ, R. A. (1945) Hospitalism: an enquiry into the genesis of psychiatric conditions in early childhood, in *Psychoanalytic Study of the Child*, **1**, 53–74; **2**, 113–17.

STEVENS, S. S. and GALANTER, E. H. (1957) Ratio scales and category scales for a dozen perceptual continua, *J. Exptl. Psychol.* **54**, 377–411.

SUTHERLAND, N. S. (1964) Visual discrimination in animals, *Brit. Med. Bull.* **20**, 54–9.

TAFT, L. T. and GOLDFARB, W. (1964) Prenatal and perinatal factors in childhood schizophrenia, *Dev. Med. Child. Neurol.* **6**, 32–43.

TATERKA, J. H. and KATZ, J. (1955) Study of correlations between electroencephalographic and psychological patterns in emotionally disturbed children, *Psychosom. Med.* **17**, 62–72.

TEMPLIN, M. C. (1957) *Certain Language Skills in Children: their development and interrelationships*, University of Minnesota Press, Minneapolis.

TUBBS, V. K. (1966) Types of linguistic disability in psychotic children, *J. Ment. Def. Res.* **10**, 230–40.

VAN KREVELEN, D. A. (1952) Early infantile autism, *Acta Paedopsychiat.* **30**, 303–23.

VEDANEV, R. P. and KARMANOVIA, I. G. (1958) On the comparative physiology of the orienting reflex, in *The Orienting Reflex and Exploratory Behaviour*, A. V. Voronin (Ed.), Acad. Pedag. Sci., Moscow.

VENABLES, P. H. (1968) Experimental psychological studies of chronic schizophrenia, in *Studies in Psychiatry*, M. Shepherd and D. L. Davies (Eds.), Oxford University Press, London.

VENABLES, P. H. and MARTIN, I. (1967) Skin resistance and skin potential, in *A Manual of Psychophysiological Methods*, P. H. Venables and I. Martin (Eds.), North-Holland Publishing Co., Amsterdam.

WALK, R. D. and GIBSON, E. J. (1959) A study of visual perception in the human infant with a visual cliff, in *Scientific American* (Paper read at East Psychol. Assoc., Atlantic City, N.J. April).

WALTERS, R. H. and PARKE, R. D. (1964) Social dependency and susceptibility to social influence, in *Advances in Experimental Social Psychology*, L. Berkowitz (Ed.), Academic Press, New York.

WALTERS, R. H. and PARKE, R. D. (1965) The role of distance receptors in the development of social responsiveness, in *Advances in Child Development and Behaviour*, **2**, 59–96, L. P. Lipsitt and C. C. Spiker (Eds.), Academic Press, New York.

WARREN, J. M. (1959) Solution of object and positional discrimination in rhesus monkeys, *J. Comp. Physiol. Psychol.* **52**, 92–3.

WARREN, J. M. (1960) Solution of sign differentiated objects and positional discrimination by rhesus monkeys, *J. Genet. Psychol.* **96**, 365–9.

WAUGH, N. C. and NORMAN, D. A. (1965) Primary memory, *Psychol. Rev.* **72**, 89–104.

WERNER, H. (1944) Development of visuo–motor performance with marble-board test in mentally retarded children, *J. Gen. Psychol.* **64**, 268–89.

WHITE, B. L., CASTLE, P. and HELD, R. (1964) Observations on the development of visually directed reaching, *Child Devel.* **35**, 349–64.

WHITE, B. L. and HELD, R. (1966) Plasticity of sensori–motor development in the human infant, in *The Causes of Behaviour: readings in child development and educational psychology*, G. J. F. Rosenblith and W. Allinsmith (Eds.), Allyn & Bacon Inc., Boston.

WHITE, S. H. and PLUM, G. (1962) Child's eye movements during a discrimination series, *Amer. Psychol.* **17**, 367.

WING, J. K. (1966) Diagnosis, epidemiology, aetiology, in *Childhood Autism: clinical, educational and social aspects*, J. K. Wing (Ed.), Pergamon Press, London.

WING, L. (1967) The handicaps of autistic children—results of a pilot study, in *Proceedings of the Congress of the International Association for the Scientific Study of Mental Deficiency*, B. W. Richards (Ed.), Mick & Jackson, England, pp. 505–12.

WOHLWILL, J. F. (1966) Developmental studies of perception, chapter in *Pattern Recognition*, L. Uhr (Ed.), Wiley, New York.

WOLFF, P. H. (1963) Observations on the early development of smiling, in *Determinants of Infant Behaviour*, **II**, 113–34 B. Fosse (Ed.), Wiley, New York.

WORSTER-DROUGHT, J. C. (1957) Observations on speech disorders in children, *Postgrad. Med. J.* **33**, 486–93.

ZACHINIAERA, I. A. (1950) Summation of two conditional stimuli reinforced by two alimentary unconditioned stimuli, in *Problems of Higher Nervous Activity*, P. K. Anokhin (Ed.), Acad. Med. Sci., Moscow.

ZAPOROZHETS, A. V. (1961) The origin and development of the conscious control of movements in man, in *Recent Soviet Psychology*, N. O'Connor (Ed.), Pergamon Press, Oxford.

ZEAMAN, D. and HOUSE, B. J. (1953) The role of attention in retardate discrimination learning, in *Handbook of Mental Deficiency*, N. Ellis (Ed.) McGraw-Hill, New York.

ZEAMAN, D., HOUSE, B. J. and ORLANDO, R. (1958) Use of special training conditions in visual discrimination learning with imbeciles, *Amer. J. Ment. Def.* **63**, 453–9.

ZINCHENKO, V. P. and LOMOV, B. F. (1960) *The Functions of Hand and Eye Movements in the Process of Perception*, Pergamon Press, London.